Barefoot *and* Cross-Eyed

Barefoot *and* Cross-Eyed

the Way of Christian Womanhood

DENISE DORMINY

XULON PRESS

Xulon Press
555 Winderley Pl, Suite 225
Maitland, FL 32751
407.339.4217
www.xulonpress.com

Paperback ISBN-13: 978-1-66289-390-2
Hardcover ISBN-13: 978-1-66289-391-9
eBook ISBN-13: 978-1-66289-392-6

This is for you, Mom.

For Shanna, Olivia, Jane, Josephine
and all my "daughters" to come:
May you love Jesus with all you are,
love others with all your strength,
and do what is right without being frightened by any fear.

This is your God-given legacy.
Just be faithful Christians, my darlings.

For Jon, Jonathon and Luke:
my mighty men who love well.

Lord, whom have I in heaven but You? And besides You I desire nothing on earth.

My flesh and my heart may fail, but You are the strength of my heart and my portion forever. Your nearness is my good. I have made You my refuge that I may tell of all Your works.

(From Psalm 73:25-26,28)

Table of Contents

Introduction

I was reminded by a friend that explanations and bios are for back covers. Maybe so. But introductions are for introducing, and an explanation might be in order before you, reader, invest your precious time in the words to follow.

Charles Spurgeon wrote: "…I resorted to my pen as an available means of doing good. I would have preached had I been able, but as my Master denied me the privilege of thus serving Him, I gladly avail myself of the other method of bearing testimony for His name. O that He may give me fruit in this field also, and His shall be all the praise."[1] Spurgeon was kept from preaching by "protracted illness and weakness." I'm kept from preaching by my gender. I'm cool with it. I'm a joyful complementarian. This book is a means of doing good, of partly fulfilling my responsibility as an older woman in the church. In doing so, I'm making a few assumptions of which you might want to be aware.

I assume you, reader, are a Christian woman. I have generations of women in view, those who walk before me, and those coming behind, young and old. Years ago (and even now) I needed, well, a *me*. Someone my *now* age or older. Most of the older Christian women who mentored me did so unknowingly through their books, most often pretty old and dusty ones. Every Timothea needs a Paulette, if you follow me. We don't grow in Christ like so many stalks of corn in a row. Rather we grow in community. We are branches in a vine, weaving in and out and around one another, drawing strength from the vine, producing fruit, but ever connected to one another

---

[1] Charles H. Spurgeon, *The Treasury of David* (London, Edinburgh, New York: Marshall Brothers Publishers), Vol. I,vi.

because we are connected to Jesus. Daughters need their mothers. Younger women need older women.

Our current culture doesn't make this easy for us. Women often find their peers or Google a more present help. In a world that is so information saturated, we are bound to find a few bitter wells from which to draw. The feminism well calls women to grab for rights and work to keep them. Social media calls us toward promiscuity, public navel-gazing, greed, and envy. Ads offer the well of eternal youth and shame us for keeping our pounds, gray hair, and laugh lines. Doctors and psychologists take public stages trying to convince us that "me time" and "self-care" are sacred. All of life appears to be centered on what we think we deserve, how to get what we want when we want it and the way we want it. Even Christian women, if they are not sipping from those bitter wells, are running to videos and conferences and books for do-it-yourself quick fixes for whatever ails them. They are hoping to hear a voice able to tame their desires and discontentment and turn them into a "somebody." Ear-tickling abounds from many "evangeligirls." These wells are not necessarily bad in themselves, but as a replacement for the only real and present help, Christ and His church, women end up isolated and defeated.

I also assume, like me, you want to learn what it means to *live* like a Christian woman. The Bible instructs older women to teach younger women in areas of character and conduct fit for women of God. Though there are many Christian resources at our fingertips, we easily overlook the resources sitting next to us in the pew. Older women know things.

I described this book as my means of doing good. I can be the older woman next to you in the pew because I've been the younger woman floundering for spiritual footing. So many of my early years were spent in search of the kind of life I have now. You can learn from my mistakes as much as you can learn from what I now know. By no means do I have it all together. I'm a rescued waif. I like the word *waif*. It's what I was before Christ found me – a stray; a neglected wretch. Now I'm a barefoot, sometimes limping or crawling, Christian waif. I've kicked off my shoes because the ground is holy, and I've met the God who is both to be feared and enjoyed. I walk like a Christian, with feet that are dirty, then clean, then dirty, then clean. I'm a saved waif – a wide-eyed, cross-eyed 62-year-old wild child resolved to keep my eyes fixed on the One who pulled me out of a pit and set me in a broad place just because He delighted in me (Ps. 18:19). He has graciously tuned my ears to His word. I hope to share with you the simple two-step of the Christian life. A rhythm. A dance I've learned. It's the "swag" of the redeemed. Repent, believe. Repent, believe. Like a waif begging in the streets, I have nothing to offer you except what I've been given. God assures me that He is enough. In order to get in step with this rhythm, we have to know the truth, then repent of our own ways, believing God's word to us. We do what we believe. Truth first, then the trek.

It's long overdue for us to mutually care for one another, old to young, young to old, and prove the word of God to be beautiful and right and perfect. It's time we flagrantly delight in and live out God's design for His daughters, humbly embracing who we truly are according to the truth of God's word. What are God's women supposed to look like? He has graciously given us a quick guide – you know, the kind that will take me 16 chapters to barely plumb the depths, and a lifetime for us to dig out all the jewels and wear them. Here is God's own description of Christian women:

> *Older women likewise are to be reverent in their behavior, not malicious gossips nor enslaved to much wine, teaching what is good, so that they may encourage the young women to love their husbands, to love their children, to be sensible, pure, workers at home, kind, being subject to their own husbands, so that the word of God will not be dishonored. Titus 2:3-5*

> *In the same way, you wives, be submissive to your own husbands so that even if any of them are disobedient to the word, they may be won without a word by the behavior of their wives, as they observe your chaste and respectful behavior. Your adornment must not be merely external – braiding the hair, and wearing gold jewelry, or putting on dresses; but let it be the*

> *hidden person of the heart, with the imperishable quality of a gentle and quiet spirit, which is precious in the sight of God. For in this way in former times the holy women also, who hoped in God, used to adorn themselves, being submissive to their own husbands; just as Sarah obeyed Abraham, calling him lord, and you have become her children if you do what is right without being frightened by any fear. 1 Pet. 3:1-6*

Here's the thing – we must be what we are. Not just women, but distinctly Christian women if we want to see God's kingdom grow and flourish. The wells of the world are broken cisterns in sharp contrast to the refreshing, ever-flowing fountain of Christ exhibited in His church. Young or old, we need one another. As we examine the Bible's picture of Christian womanhood, I pray you will kick off your shoes and set your eyes on Jesus and His gospel, and allow the rhythm of repentance and faith to guide your feet. It's a cleansing, transforming rhythm of the Holy Spirit working His purpose into us, changing us from glory to glory, as we taste and see through Scripture that God is indeed good and good to each of us. So, my friends, sit next to me on this pew, and let's look at God's design for you and me. Let's turn from our own way and, by faith, choose the Way to life. Onward and upward, daughters of the King![2]

---

[2] A snarky wave to Jen Hatmaker who thinks "the King's daughters are THE WORST. I only want to hang out with the King's kitchen staff, because his internet daughters are mean as the Devil's hell." Apparently, to criticize is to be a pharisaical jerk. Jen Hatmaker, *Fierce, Free and Full of Fire: the Guide to Being Glorious You.* (Nashville, TN: Nelson Books, 2020), pg. 24. Though I'm citing the quote, I don't recommend reading it – there's not a bit of Bible in it.

Chapter 1

Barefoot and Cross-Eyed

As I'm writing this, I've got my bare feet propped up on a stool. Rain is pelting the roof of my back porch, and I am musing over John 13. Muse with me:

> *Now before the Feast of the Passover, Jesus knowing that His hour had come that He would depart out of this world to the Father, having loved His own who were in the world, He loved them to the end. During supper, the devil having already put into the heart of Judas Iscariot, the son of Simon, to betray Him, Jesus, knowing that the Father had given all things into His hands, and that He had come forth from God and was going back to God, got up from supper, and laid aside His garments; and taking a towel, He girded Himself. Then He poured water into the basin, and began to wash the disciples' feet and to wipe them with the towel with which He was girded. So He came to Simon Peter. He said to Him, "Lord, do You wash my feet?" Jesus answered and said to him, "What I do you do not realize now, but you will understand hereafter." Peter said to Him, "Never shall You wash my feet!" Jesus answered him, "If I do not wash you, you have no part with Me." Simon Peter said to Him, "Lord, then wash not only my feet, but also my hands and my head." Jesus said to him, "He who has bathed needs only to wash his feet, but is completely clean; and you*

> *are clean, but not all of you." For He knew the one who was betraying Him; for this reason He said, "Not all of you are clean." John 13:1-11*

Before you think Peter a little ridiculous, put yourself in the room with him. Who should be kneeling before whom? Peter is fully aware of who Jesus is and who he himself is not. God? Washing my feet? But then Jesus makes it clear that if Peter wants Christ, he needs a washing. Peter is all in. Look at his response! Head to toe, then, Lord! All of me! I'm Yours. Jesus says, "Just your feet. You are already clean." And so it is with Christians. We are already clean. When Jesus saves us, He washes us completely. We are new. And we stay that way. It's just that our daily walk through the world gets our feet a bit dirty. Daily sin, therefore, daily repentance - this is the way of faith. We are dependent upon Jesus as much for the daily removal of sin as we are for the complete cleansing and forgiveness of our sins when we are first saved. Peter saw this. He was barefoot and cross-eyed. Shoes off and ready for the washtub. Eyes trained on the face of Jesus. Repentant and believing. This is the "how" of growing in Christ. It's the divine rhythm of the Christian life. Repent. Believe. Repent. Believe.

The writer of Hebrews puts it this way: "...let us also *lay aside every encumbrance and the sin which so easily entangles us* [barefoot, repentant], and let us run with endurance the race that is set before us, *fixing our eyes on Jesus,* the author and perfecter of faith [cross-eyed, believing]" (Heb. 12:1-2).[3]

The Bible has many ways of describing the continual war that we wage against sin. Paul tells us in Romans 6 to "consider yourselves to be dead to sin, but alive to God in Christ Jesus" and to "not let sin reign in your mortal body so that you obey its lusts" (Ro. 6: 11-12). He reminds us to "not go on presenting the members of your body to sin as instruments of unrighteousness; but present yourselves to God as those alive from the dead, and your members as instruments of righteousness to God" (Ro. 6:13). Paul uses the

---

[3] Italics and brackets mine.

language of putting the old aside and putting on the new (Eph. 4:20-24, Col. 3:9-10). John Owen would tell us to mortify (or kill) sin and to vivify (live out) the virtues of the Spirit. Jesus tells us, "If your right eye makes you stumble, tear it out and throw it from you" or "if your right hand makes you stumble, cut it off and throw it from you" (Matt. 5:29-30). We are not to show our sin any pity, but to act violently toward it. Kill it.

All this is done in the power of the Holy Spirit. There is no taming sin. God does not enlist us into some sort of divine self-improvement program. For the Christian, the only sin we "kill" is the sin that Christ has already killed on the cross. His death becomes our death. His burial our burial. And His victory over sin and the grave becomes ours. We consider ourselves dead to sin because in Christ we *are* dead to sin. We consider ourselves alive to God in Christ Jesus because we *are* alive in Him. Sin is no longer our master. Jesus is. We don't deal gently with our sin. No, we treat our flesh as the treasonous enemy it is and take away sin's life. Galatians 5:16 reads, "But I say, walk by the Spirit, and you will not carry out the desire of the flesh." So many of us get the cart before the horse. We reinterpret it to say, "Stop carrying out the desire of the flesh, and you will walk by the Spirit." We think we must stop so that the Spirit will take over. But apart from Christ, we can do nothing. Apart from the Spirit's empowerment, we are impotent to even repent of one sin. Our repentance begins with Him (2 Tim. 2:25). J. I. Packer defines repentance this way:

> *Repentance, in the broadest sense, signifies that change of mind, purpose, attitude, and behavior whereby we embrace God's agenda of mercy toward us and turn back from the old life of fighting God by playing God to live the new life of humbly and thankfully serving Him. Repentance is thus a whole-person business in which a pattern of self-centered self-service is replaced by a God-centered habit of seeking others' welfare, and pride and willfulness give way to prayer and worship.*[4]

[4] J. I. Packer, *Taking God Seriously* (Wheaton, IL: Crossway, 2013), 74.

And then again, citing the Shorter Westminster Catechism:

> *Repentance unto life is a saving grace, whereby a sinner, out of a true sense of his sin, and apprehension of the mercy of God in Christ, doth, with grief and hatred of his sin, turn from it unto God, with full purpose of, and endeavour after, new obedience.*[5]

We can see from these definitions, repentance and faith working together. We are always turning from sin and turning to God for help and new life. We bare our feet for the washing, understanding our impotence to defeat sin on our own. We confess it and kill it by the power of the Holy Spirit, and by faith we turn our face fully to Christ to walk in obedience. This demands that we neither quench the Holy Spirit or grieve Him. We quench Him when we plug our ears and ignore His voice speaking to us through His word. Like water thrown on a fire, we douse the fiery words of the Lord with our own reasoning and excuses. To grieve Him is to hear Him, know exactly what He commands, and then treasonously choose our own way. We choose to be hellions and choose against our new nature in Christ. In other words, we try to do God's work our own way. No, better to be barefoot and cross-eyed, humbly repenting and by faith beholding Christ as our only hope. This is the rhythm of our daily walk in Christ. Repent. Believe. Repent. Believe.

Why start here, with repentance and faith, in a book designed to define Christian womanhood? I suppose because it's the memo I didn't get when I first became a Christian. I was told what I should be, but not *how* to be. I was a striver, not an abider. My friend and I often joke about "striving to abide." It's like saying, "I'm working really hard to rest." I've learned that repentance and faith are the key to being all Christ designed us to be. Every young woman needs to get the memo. As we have received Christ, so we are to walk in Him (Col. 2:6). How have we received Him? By grace through faith (Eph. 2:8). Titus 2:11-12 tells us that "the grace of God has

---

[5] Ibid, 78.

appeared, bringing salvation to all men, instructing us to deny ungodliness and worldly desires and to live sensibly, righteously and godly in the present age." Deny and live. Repent and believe. Grace is our instructor. As we look at the virtues of a distinctively Christian woman, our goal is to take off what displeases God and to put on what pleases Him. This takes grace, humility and faith. We are to be a bunch of barefoot and cross-eyed women. We stand on the holy ground of God's word, humbly renouncing all of our own futile ways and sins and then, with faith, we look to Christ as the source of our strength, our life, and our obedience.

I like to think of Titus 2:3-5 (and Proverbs 31), the frame of this book, as a woman in full bloom. Each flower is what the root – the source – says it is. The flower you become will not look like the flower I become, but we are certain to all manifest a resemblance to the source who gives life to each of us. Fully bloomed, we will each be reverent, truth-speaking, temperate, self-controlled, kind, sensible, pure, teachers of good who love our families, work at home, and submit to God, His word, and our earthly authorities. We will be this because we are planted in Christ. We will be this because Christ is this. Repentance and faith are the means of appropriating all that we already are in Him.

It's my prayer that the following chapters will not just be descriptive of an ideal Christian woman. Rather, I pray that they will remind you, if you belong to Christ, this is who you are, now, in Him. Inside the acorn is an oak tree. "For you have died and your life is hidden with Christ in God. When Christ, who is our life, is revealed, then you also will be revealed with Him in glory" (Col. 3:3-4). It's an already-not-yet life that we live. Who we are is who we are daily becoming. So, "lay aside every encumbrance and the sin which so easily entangles us." Repent. And "let us run with endurance the race that is set before us, fixing our eyes on Jesus, the author and perfecter of faith." Believe.

Barefoot. Cross-eyed. Let's strive to abide and become who we are.

Chapter 2

Fashioned for Glory

I love jigsaw puzzles. I especially like the kind with no borders and extra pieces. When the puzzle is complete, I like to leave it out for a few days to revel in the wonder that at least one thing in my life is finished. But there, in the box, lay several pieces that have no place. Extras. They serve no real purpose other than to confound us as we fit the rest together. Have you ever felt like a piece without a place? Like you don't fit and you only seem to confound the lives around you?

That's descriptive of most of my life. The girl who didn't fit. And I wanted to... desperately. From a very young age, I was on a quest for the thing that would make me mean something. I was a waif, a beggar, holding out my emotional cup and hoping someone, anyone, would affirm that I had a place, that I had meaning, that if I hadn't been born, there would be at least an infinitesimal breach in the cosmos. Without a sense of purpose and belonging, desperation sends us into some dark places. Like a pinball, we get batted to and fro, from one dashed hope to another, searching for a place to land, to fit. I spent a good bit of my life batted around and groping in the dark.

If there was one, I could probably get a "Failure to Fit Award" for the multiple times I've attempted to chameleon my way through life. I adopted the philosophy of "if it don't fit – force it" through most of my adolescence. That is, I pretended to fit. Who I was depended upon who I was with. I tried so hard to be what I thought others wanted me to be that I didn't have an original thought. I didn't know what I truly believed. I didn't know what I liked. My fear was that if anyone looked close enough, they would discover that I didn't fit anywhere at all, that I was designed to be unlovable, thrown into the lid of the puzzle box, separate and useless, an imposter, a faker.[6]

Designed to Fit

Imagine my surprise when God opened my eyes to see I am truly fashioned for a purpose, uniquely designed to fit. It is a wonder – things into which angels long to look. He fashioned me into a woman, and He fashioned me into a Christ-follower. Christians are fit for a new life, one with God-given rules and roles, one with balanced liberty, one with unspeakable joy and purpose. We are born by grace through faith in Jesus Christ to be part of His body, the church, with Christ as the head. And each of us is fitted for His particular purpose in His particular plan where He has particularly placed us. No one else can "do you" in God's kingdom. God made me to be me. God made you to be you. And He made us, as believers in Christ, to be fit into that same body, working out our salvation for His glory. What a relief! We don't have to force fit ourselves into this world or into God's kingdom. He has placed us – fit us – and given us uniquely designed roles under His rule. This is not only true in the church, but true in our relationships and in our homes as well.

Amos was two. We sat in the floor with a Chinese Checkers board and various pieces from other board games dumped and spread hither and yon, everything from chessmen to pachisi pieces to jackstraws. He was endeavoring to fit the various pieces into the shallow holes fashioned for marbles. I was tickled by his facial expressions. He went from bemused to perplexed to frustrated to "I've had enough!" Destruction was inevitable, so I handed him a marble. It fit. He matched the blue marble to the blue triangle and

---

[6] I've since come to understand that this behavior is not completely insane. Shame, fear, and insecurity – no matter the core reasons – are favorite tools of the Christian's enemies (flesh, world, the adversary), but they find their destruction at the cross as much as any sin. Shout out to the late Brennan Manning whose book *Abba's Child: The Cry of the Heart for Intimate Belonging* brought healing in this area. (Colorado Springs, CO: NavPress, 1994)

placed it in a hole. His expression changed to sheer delight. With a toddler's precision, he placed marble after marble into the proper holes. Playful contentment resumed.

God, in His wonder and wisdom, spoke the world and all that is in it into existence. With divine intention, He fashioned all things to work in specific ways for specific reasons. He fashioned man out of dirt from the ground and brought him to life by heavenly breath. Adam was told "to work and keep the garden" (Gen. 2:15). God said, "It is not good for the man to be alone; I will make him a helper suitable [fit] for him" (Gen. 2:18). In the text, instead of moving right to divine surgery and Eve's creation, God parades beasts and birds in front of Adam to name. Then we read this: "But for Adam there was not found a helper suitable for him" (Gen. 2:20b). Like Amos, nothing fit. Zebra? No. Kangaroo? Nope. Hyena? Definitely not. When the last beast walked off with a name, God handed over the "marble." "So the LORD God caused a deep sleep to fall upon the man, and he slept; then He took one of his ribs and closed up the flesh at that place. The LORD God fashioned into a woman the rib which He had taken from the man, and brought her to the man" (Genesis 2:21-22). Woman was fashioned by the very hand of God for a man, for a specific reason, a divine fitting.

What if a woman doesn't want to be an Eve? What if the pachisi piece is no longer fulfilled by pachisi-ing? Can it take the queen's place on the chessboard? Sure. But frankly, if I was playing chess, that pachisi piece would drive me nuts. It needs to stay in the game for which it was created. The world right now is filled with people trying to play the queen, out of place, refusing to stay in their God-designed role. Men want to be women and swim on the women's swim team. Men are "marrying" men. Women are "marrying" women. Gay men are buying children via surrogates. Women aren't *fulfilled* unless they are out of their homes, away from their kids, leaving anyone else to diaper baby number three. Grown men (stuck in boyhood) are living in their parents' basements, staying on pop's cell phone plan, and setting up gaming caves. Or they are marrying and sending their wives to work while they learn to make bread and play video games at home. Children are attempting to parent their parents, ruling their homes with violent entitlement. Grandparents are parenting their grandchildren out of worry and guilt. It's crazy out there. It's like going to the concessions at a football game. Why doesn't everyone just get in a line? What's a woman to do?

The better question is: What's a Christian woman to do? What is her God-designed lane? What were we made to be? What were we made to do? Are we only fit, as the old (and contemptuous) adage describes, to be kept barefoot and pregnant? Or are we made to "bring home the bacon, fry it up in a pan, and never let you forget you're a man?"[7] Will we be unfulfilled if we've never toted signs in a march for equal rights, equal pay, and the right to be "nasty"[8] or mutilate or kill our children? Does every movie really have to showcase a woman superhero with her pansy male friend?[9] It's possible Christian women have misunderstood or simply missed God's plan for their greatest satisfaction and hope.

Helper? Is that all?

My husband and I dated in the early 1980s. I was working full time and living in an apartment. He liked that I earned my own money. I liked that I earned my own money. Independence, as in our current culture, was highly esteemed. I thought being a strong, independent woman would help me to fit, to be accepted. My husband liked it until he didn't. God wrecked our plans by stepping in and taking over. Suddenly independence was *passé* and dependence on Jesus Christ and on one another was *vogue*. I was face to face with a new concept: I was designed to be a helper. Frankly, I didn't much like it.

It doesn't seem particularly commendable to be christened a *helper* by your Maker. I'm a helper? In other words, I'm second violinist in the

---

7 From an old *Enjoli* perfume commercial with a sultry woman in a business suit holding a frying pan – the "8 hour perfume for the 24 hour woman."

8 This references a poem read by Ashley Judd at a 2017 Women's march.

9 I'm getting a little steamed. My apologies. We've just met.

orchestra, not good enough for first chair? I'm not the winner, so I'm the loser. When I hear *helper*, I'm reminded of my dad's instruction, "Dennie, a good helper anticipates. Pay attention. Know what I need before I need it and have the tool ready." I don't feel warm and fuzzy with dad's interpretation. Is a helper really someone who reads minds and hands the important dude a tool? Many of us quickly put helper in the *slave* or *wannabe* grouping. The lie is that helpers are there only *in case*. This is not the biblical use of *helper*. God never intended the title as an insult. And it's not one.

"Then the LORD God said, 'It is not good for the man to be alone; I will make him a helper suitable for him'" (Gen. 2:18). One of the more obvious things to consider about a helper is simply that you can't be one without someone. The first *not good* thing recorded in Scripture was man's solitude, his *aloneness*. To say it positively, it's good for man to have a helper, and not just any helper, but a helper suited to him. A woman. Eve was the female prototype uniquely fashioned as a counterpart for Adam. Created female, she is still in the image of God and, in her union with Adam, she becomes a picture of the bride in union with Christ. This being true, whether you are a woman or a Christian woman, your original hardwiring is to be a fit helper as a bride. In fact, the Hebrew word translated as *helper* can be better understood as *strong helper*. It is used to describe military reinforcements, the kind without which a battle would be lost. It is also used in the Bible most often to describe God Himself as our strong help (cf. Ex. 18:4, Ps. 33:20). God is saying that women are necessary helpers, not simply afterthoughts.

No Plan B

Have you ever felt like God's plan B? I have. Once I was asked to take the place of a notable conference speaker who was unavoidably detained. I took her place as the Friday night keynote speaker. I remember teaching, singing, and leaving the conference that night sick to my stomach, feeling as though I let everyone down. I didn't stay to hear the fallout. I was the afterthought. "She can't make it, so we thought of you..." The next day I went to hear the scheduled speaker teach. She was as engaging and encouraging as her books. I thought, "I'm so sorry the ladies got me instead of her last night." A few minutes later, a young woman approached me, handed me a slip of paper, and walked off. It said, "You were not God's plan B last night. You WERE the plan." My mouth dropped open.

I'm not God's plan B in my marriage either. Neither are you. You are the plan, not an afterthought. If you are married, you are the one God chose for the man you married, at least once the knot was tied. It might be hard, but it's the plan. God deals in plan As. Indeed, Adam needed Eve. And Eve was fit for Adam in the sense that she corresponded to him. She was equal in dignity, value and worth, and uniquely fitted to complement him and aide him in his ordained purpose and call. We are co-dominion takers.

This is God's design. Unfortunately, the prototype was distorted at the fall. Not lost, but corrupted, misshapen, and twisted. When sin entered the world, man and woman could no longer perfectly image their Creator. Because of their sin, which is our own sin, neither can we. It's important to remember that God was not surprised. Before the foundation of the world, the cross of Jesus Christ was already in full view. The theme of the Bible was written: "Kill the dragon; Get the girl."[10] Christ has crushed the head of the serpent. The girl, the Bride, has been secured with His blood. Marriage between two Christians (male and female) is meant to put the covenant relationship of Christ and His church on display to the rest of the world. It's meant to show that you, Christian, are securely connected (fitted) to the head, who is Christ Jesus.

I was sitting in a hair salon, hair wet and ready to cut, chatting with a young woman from Pakistan. Scissors in hand, she told me about her husband, of their separation that could only happen in the United States, her new-found "freedom" to be a successful woman, and then she said, "My mother taught me that marriage is a duty and that love doesn't matter." I replied, "Love matters. It's who God is. Did you know God actually

---

[10] This succinct descriptor of the whole Bible narrative came to my attention through Douglas Wilson. I'm told it originated in one of his expositions and that Joe Rigney devised the theme itself. However it came about, it was not original with me and I'm crazy about it.

commands my husband to love me? Marriage is a covenant and love matters. In fact, I'm my husband's glory and crown – this hair right here is a picture of it." She stared at me in the mirror and then said, "How much of your glory do you want me to cut off?" And she stopped sharing. I get it. Touchy subject. The point is Christian marriages picture a far greater reality, the love of a compassionate God for a flawed people, and a redeemed people loving and serving God. The dragon, Satan, is defeated, and Christ has secured His girl, the church. The Eve prototype has been and is being restored. Woman is her husband's glory and crown.

Glory and Crown

The woman as helper is not some fragile little porcelain doll for the mantlepiece. When a man wins a woman, he is, according to the Bible, being glorified (1 Cor. 11:7b). A wedding is a man's coronation day. He gets a strong helper, and he gets a crown. "An excellent wife is the crown of her husband" (Prov. 12:4a). Since God has defined woman in relation to a man, being a helper and crown is in the blueprint. This is a bit like a woman's make and model. "But I want you to understand that Christ is the head of every man, and the man is the head of a woman, and God is the head of Christ" (1 Cor. 11:3). Later we read that "man is the image and glory of God; but the woman is the glory of man" (1 Cor. 11:7b). Hop on the authority train with me for a moment:

Woman → *her head is* **Man** → *his head is* **Christ** → Christ's head is **God**

God is not saying man is worth more than woman. In fact, He is making a scandalously beautiful statement. If man is the glory of God, then woman is the glory of the glory. One pastor called her "the shining dome on the capital building." I prefer the icing on the cake, the sprinkles on the donut, the wool on the sheep. I should have stopped. We will consider more about headship in a later chapter. For now, I ask you to consider the extraordinary nature of your God-inspired design. Just as Jesus submitted to the Father while He walked this earth, though equal with the Father, He "did not regard equality with God a thing to be grasped, but emptied Himself, taking the form of a bond-servant," so a wife is privileged to mirror this same Jesus (Php. 2:5-11). We women can breathe easy as helpers and crowns because our allegiance is first of all to Jesus and to follow His example is just downright lovely.

Kingdom Builders

> *God created man in His own image, in the image of God He created him; male and female He created them. God blessed them; and God said to them, "Be fruitful and multiply, and fill the earth, and subdue it; and rule over the fish of the sea and over the birds of the sky and over every living thing that moves on the earth. Genesis 1:27-18*

Though the image of God in mankind was corrupted by sin at the fall, this didn't change the vocation Adam and Eve were given. They were given an assignment. They were to be fruitful, multiply, fill the earth, subdue the earth, and rule over every living thing. Even after the fall, Genesis 3:23 tells us "The LORD God sent him [Adam] out from the garden of Eden, to cultivate the ground from which he was taken." He didn't cease to do the work God commanded him; it was just much harder. Eve would be fruitful and multiply, but her pain in childbirth was greatly multiplied and her desire would be for her husband and her husband would rule over her (Gen. 3:16). Same jobs. Tougher working conditions. The commission is still the same. We populate the world with children of the covenant. We war in prayer and song every Sunday and take dominion throughout the week. We work hard in our communities. And we obey the words of our Lord before He was taken into heaven: "Go therefore and make disciples of all the nations, baptizing them in the name of the Father and the Son and the Holy Spirit, teaching them to observe all that I commanded you; and lo, I am with you always, even to the end of the age" (Matt. 28:19-20). We subdue the earth until it is "filled with the knowledge of the glory of the LORD, as the waters cover the sea" (Hab. 2:14).

Our family meals are at the top of my greatest pleasures. I have three children who married and multiplied. We are eighteen around the table, eight adults and ten children. So many olive plants with hands and voices raised in praise and heads bowed in prayer, that my gratitude takes my breath away. In a small way, we are God's architecture, a microcosm of His glorious kingdom, fruit of a fruitful vine, the beauty of laboring, subduing hands, the blessing of the Lord on undeserving children who were given grace. I see it almost daily.

Sometimes, in the moments before they arrive or after they leave, I remember how it could have gone. God could have left me to my own devices. Trajectories are fast and easy under the feet of sinful people. We are easily moved by foolish decisions and worldly pressure, by self-protection and selfish leisure. Apart from God, the architecture would have been a monument to my own foolishness, with my husband and children paying dearly for it. The blessing of God on us is not because of us; it is because of Christ's faithfulness to uphold His word, to do what He promised. I believe this is one of the secrets of kingdom building. We learn to build for the right reasons. When we build for ourselves, the result is a tower of Babel, temporary and marked for demolition. When we trust God to build the house, and we obey the blueprint, blessing is inevitable.

Foolishness Isn't Help

We women are helpers, but it is possible to be lousy ones, unproductive and foolish. I know this from experience. At the beginning of my marriage, I tried to build our house on preference and convenience. We can ignore the blueprint and remove the bearing walls and watch our houses fall around us. Many Christian women are doing that even now. We can be crowns only to discover we minted them from fool's gold, pretenders and hypocrites, tinny and hollow in our faith. We can be slothful, cowardly, and selfish instead of working, subduing, multiplying, and glorifying.

Oh yeah. It can go very wrong. The way of the transgressor looks easy, but the Bible calls it "hard" (Prov. 13:15, ASV). To try to live outside the design is a recipe for disaster.

My husband took a job in Atlanta, GA in 1998. We moved from the Bible belt of Oklahoma to what I afterward dubbed "the wilderness." Culture shock is a mild term to describe our household's response to the change. We had more money than we had ever had. We had a new home in a nice neighborhood. Our children were placed in the best and largest school system in Georgia. Remember the story of the Israelites in Numbers 11? They were complaining that all they had was "this manna" and they wanted meat to eat. Because of their complaining, Moses told them God would send quail, but he added the codicil, "You shall eat, not one day, nor two days, nor five days, nor ten days, nor twenty days, but a whole month, until it comes out of your nostrils and becomes loathsome to you; because you have rejected the LORD who is among you and have wept before Him, saying, 'Why did we ever leave Egypt?'" (Num. 11:19-20). Or did he say Oklahoma? We connected to a megachurch, one where no one saw us come and no one saw us go. We never made one friend there. Our children hated Sunday School. Immorality poured into our home like water into holes of a sinking ship. One of my sons even asked me, "Mom, do you even like God anymore?" There couldn't be a bigger red flag than that! Because of our lack of need, we scrapped our dependence on God. Our "blessings" became loathsome to us. Our children rebelled. Eventually, we came around, helped plant a church in a nearby city with an old friend, and as soon as we were given the opportunity, we got the heck out of Dodge and started over. The years there were an experiment in living according to our own design, abandoning the blueprint. We spiraled. Truth be known, we almost choked the life out of our marriage and family. When we ignore God's design, we women can pull the house down around us. God was gracious to us and gave my husband a job opportunity in what we now call "the promised land."

Glory on Display

In God's grace, we women are uniquely fashioned, built for a distinct calling and offered an opportunity to display the glory of Jesus in ways that men cannot. I love the words of Elisabeth Eliott: "The fact that I am a woman does not make me a different kind of Christian, but the fact that I am a Christian does make me a different kind of woman. For I have accepted God's idea of me, and my whole life is an offering back to Him of all that I am and all that He wants me to be."[11] That's it, isn't it? To put a fine point on it: just be a Christian, woman.

The role God designed for us fits us. We can be comfortable in our God-given placement. Freedom in Christ means we are free to be who He intended us to be and free to do what He intended us to do. Contentment comes from this kind of freedom. May I admonish you? Do the right thing for the right reason in the right way. Let God's truth determine your trajectory, not the current culture, tradition, feelings, pressures, or even your past. Take advice from a woman who didn't fit, but has now been placed firmly in her God-given place. Just be a Christian. Jesus set the bar high. We sit where He sits, after all (Eph. 2:6). As a Christian, God "has given us everything we need for life and godliness through the true knowledge of Him who called us" (2 Pet. 1:3).

Full disclosure. When Jon and I first married, our vows represented our wrong understanding of life and our roles in it. Granted we were blind to Christ. Our god was selfishness. We wrote our own vows which could have easily been interpreted, "I will kinda sorta like you, if you will kinda sorta like me." I am not exaggerating. To my shame, I edited 1 Corinthians 13. Our vows were indicative of our flimsy commitment and our own hubris, our desire to stand alone together. We were slaves of our appetites and the only thing we were fit for was destruction. God's people have been corrupted by sin, but His design is still perfect. And in Him, the necessary renovation is being made. There is indeed a grand design, but it is the arms

[11] Elisabeth Elliot, *Let Me Be A Woman* (Illinois: Tyndale House, 1976).

of faith that embrace it. Being stiff-necked and force fitting our own ways onto God's design never works. What *does* work is humble repentance and childlike trust. We renounce our independence and submit to God's hand, accepting our God-given roles by faith instead of kicking against them.[12]

Can you imagine the joy of a life that has completely embraced its purpose – to glorify God and enjoy Him forever? That joy is contingent upon our humbly accepting His will for us as Christian women and refusing to find our hope outside of Him. We are fashioned for eternity, so let's move in that direction.

[12] When God changed our hearts, we renewed our marriage vows. Incidentally, I asked the pastor for the longest, strictest vows he could find. I thought it fit with my repentance. He was glad to oblige.

Chapter 3

So You Want to Be Equal?

Older women ***likewise…***
Titus 2:3a

Likewise

You might be thinking, "She wants us to look at God's design for Christian womanhood but starts with *likewise?*" I can't think of a more important place to start.

I live near the epicenter of our government. Washington, DC is about an hour from me. Fifteen years ago, I was clamoring to drag everyone I knew to visit the monuments, the museums, the Library of Congress, the National Archives. I love art. I love history. I was in awe, and I wanted others to be in awe. Now, between the rhetoric and the rallies for rights – those rights, my rights, her rights, black, purple, blue, pink, and rainbow rights – I've become a mite jaded. And saddened. The last women's rights rally hurled me over the edge. No, I didn't attend. The central theme seemed to be "Give us everything. We deserve it."

If you were to pop in on the webpage for NOW (the National Organization for Women Foundation), you would discover why the central theme of women's rights is confusing. These are their core issues as of 2023: Reproductive rights and justice (translation, "I get to kill my baby"), economic justice, ending violence against women, racial justice,[13] LGBTQUIA+ rights,[14] and constitutional equality (which, by the way, women already have). How did all of these issues get swept under the umbrella of women's rights? To painfully over-simplify, this appears to be a whine. "Life ain't fair and I want everyone and everything to be the same for everybody unless it makes me unhappy. Your rights only matter if they matter to me." Do they have some good points? A few. Women's suffrage has been helpful throughout our history. I like that I get to vote, and I think women should. I think men should stop beating their wives (and wives should stop beating their husbands). We can agree on some things, but how we go about those changes just might not include wearing a pink vagina hat and carrying a "Grab 'Em by the Patriarchy" sign. My outrage is far greater than one or two good points.

Why bring this up? Because bad ideas from years of popular social media sites and major media outlets bled into the church. Are you "woke" yet? At the risk of being labeled a fossil, I'm outraged at the influx of worldly ideas that have found a canal into the church fount and specifically into the minds of her women. Do you really want to be equal with men when you have been so gloriously designed as a woman? What does the Bible teach about equality between the sexes? How do we think rightly about our roles without flinching every time the word *patriarchy* is mentioned? I think we can start with *likewise*.

Standing side-by-side, men and women in the church have a lot more *likewise* than *no-nos* and hand slaps. The Bible really does say, "There is neither Jew nor Greek, there is neither slave nor free man, there is neither male nor female; for you are all one in Christ Jesus" (Gal. 3:28). We are all

---

[13] This is their definition for racial justice: "We are constantly identifying and combating the barriers to equality and justice imposed by structural racism, particularly those that inflict a double burden of race and sex discrimination on BIPOC (Black, Indigenous, People of Color), including trans women and girls."

[14] Tutorial: Lesbian, Gay, Bisexual, Trans (trans, transexual, or transgender), Questioning or Queer, Intersex, Asexual, and the + includes – agender, demisexual, genderfluid, graysexual, non-binary/genderqueer, pansexual, omnisexual, polyamorous, sapiosexual, two-spirit… and polly-wolly-doodle-all-the-day.

sons of God through faith in Christ Jesus because we were baptized into Christ and have clothed ourselves with Christ (see Gal. 3:26-27). Did you see that? You were just called a *son* even though you are a daughter, and you lived through it. Gender, status, position, and culture mean nothing when we are in Christ. *Child of God* is the banner we fly.

Likewise, men and women are given the same gifts. God doesn't give male gifts (teaching, preaching, shepherding, administration, leading, prophecy, wisdom, knowledge, evangelism) and female gifts (faith, mercy, helps, encouragement, and hospitality). Who thinks that way! God has lavishly parceled out His gifts on His bride, giving them as He has decided best edifies His church. Do we display those gifts in the same way? The answer is no. We display those gifts (all of them) according to the image-bearer that each of us is, whether male or female. Women chafe at this. Why? One possibility is that we aren't discipled to walk in the gifts we have *as women*. Our examples are primarily men. If I have the gift of preaching or teaching or shepherding, how do I work that gift out in the context of the local church? Most of us look to our leaders who are men. We say, "Oh, Elder Joe seems to be gifted in the same way. He serves like that. That's how I'm supposed to do it." Nope. It can't work that way. Some serious "Titus-2ing" would aide us in finding our female footing.

This is why I am a huge proponent for women's discipleship. Women teachers need the opportunity to wield their sword accurately, but also in the right sphere. God didn't say women can't know what men know. Sound doctrine comes from the word, out of our pastors and teachers, to us. For women, much of the practicality of how that teaching is lived out comes from the examples and teaching of other women. That's one of the reasons for Paul's admonition to older women to train the younger. Men don't really know what it's like to be women though there are many who claim they do (and are now attempting it in high heels). How are elders to encourage women with teaching and preaching gifts, especially when we believe the Scripture clearly teaches that it doesn't look the same as the elder in the pulpit on Sunday morning?

Is It Equality We Want?

Before you set up a stake and put some brush at the foot of it, lighter in hand, I'm a firm complementarian. I don't want the pastor's mantle nor is it mine for the asking or taking. I actually do believe that elders are supposed to be men. Our greatest measure of equality is in our likeness to Christ. I know several women who believe because they match their husbands in virtue and in talent[15], their roles of service should be the same. They think I'm not far from the kingdom of God, if only I would stretch to egalitarian. But I think the Bible is clear that the office of an elder is to be held by qualified males, and I believe God's ways and His word are good, and therefore good for me (and for you, my sister in Christ). My point to this tirade: fear has crept into the Church regarding women attempting to step into offices that God did not ordain for them to hold. It's a legitimate consideration. It has happened. It would be wrong to deny that women sometimes sinfully step out of their God-ordained lanes. I simply don't believe that this "worry" precipitates an overcorrection by church leadership. We should remember women are real participants in worship, so they aren't relegated to Sunday bystanders and spectators. They need to know they are vital in their service to the Lord.

My personal stance, popular or unpopular, is that women can do anything men are allowed to do within the church ***except*** aspire to the office or serve in the office of elder. We might look at the office of elder as the tree in the garden we women aren't allowed to eat from, and for good reason – it leads to our own destruction. I don't even have a problem with women teaching men in an informal setting (see Priscilla, Acts 18:26), just not in

[15] I love you, my egalitarian pals. Lighten up, darlins!

the Lord's Service.[16] Women should seek to serve wholeheartedly in worship through song and prayer, submitting to their local church leadership, in order to serve the Lord with zeal and joy.

You won't find a stronger advocate for women's Bible literacy than I am. Women should know the Bible. Women should study the Bible. Women should pray the Bible and memorize the Bible. Women should ask their elders (and their husbands) questions related to the Bible. Women should live what the Bible teaches. Women should teach what the Bible teaches. Word, word, word everywhere. Oh, utopia! Live it and breathe it! Women need to be able to study the Bible together, one on one and in groups. They need to learn *how* to study the Bible.[17] I can't express how much spiritual growth can come from women sharpening women in a Bible study group! If God called you to teach, then teach girl, and teach well.

Several years ago, my pastor at the time asked me to meet him for coffee. I'm old enough to be his mother, so I agreed. He said, "Denise, I've been praying in regard to you, 'Lord, what do I do with this woman?'" It made me choke on my Chai. He said he recognized that I had some of the same gifts that he had and that he needed to find a place for my gifts to be used in our local church. Can I just confess? I was at once stupefied and so very grateful. He thought of me. He prayed for me. He had a list of ways for me to "help him out" writing material for small groups and teaching women's groups. He provided study resources for me[18]. I delighted to serve and never once wanted more than the liberty God had given. I know I wasn't the only

---

[16] In my younger days, before I personally settled this issue, I was asked by our pastor to teach during a Mother's Day service. The church leadership was fine with it. One congregant (not a member) wasn't. He stood up and rebuked me during the service. My children witnessed a public scolding of their mother. Though I agree with the young man now that I should not have taught during a worship service, I think he could have found a better way to oppose me than public humiliation. Just thought full disclosure was in order here.

[17] Thank you, Kay Arthur. You deepened the joy of Christ in my life through Precept Ministries by teaching me how to meet with Jesus through His word. This woman is forever grateful for you.

[18] I'm no scholar, but he treated me like one and encouraged me in my growth as a Christian.

one this discerning pastor was praying for. He remembered that half of his sheep were gifted women.[19]

Six years later, I find myself in a church that emphasizes hospitality – something at which I have to work extremely hard.[20] Our women are working in the background and doing real kingdom work. They are inviting families into their homes, fellowshipping together, homeschooling their children, preparing meals for one another. There is no structured "Women's Ministry." There are no church-supported women's Bible studies. It's easy to feel shelved by God when there is no formal place to use God-given gifts. We may feel unneeded and no longer useful to God. Truthfully, I have struggled to get my footing in this arena. Three things have helped me.

First, I was encouraged to strengthen other spiritual muscles that I previously ignored specifically *because* I'm not gifted in those areas. I do not have the gifts of mercy, service, or hospitality, but I do these things because Jesus is merciful, compassionate, and hospitable. My focus is no longer on what I'm gifted to do, but on who I'm called to serve. I want to be like Jesus. Though I believe it would be sinful to keep in a box what God gave as gifts to be used, the Bible says that the Holy Spirit has distributed His gifts to each individual as He wills, and that this same Spirit works them (1 Cor 12:11). Who are we to say to Him, "You must let me work *this* way"? It's good to be mindful that we are His workmanship, created in Christ Jesus for good works which He prepared in advance for us to do (Eph. 2:10). We dare not do what He did not prepare for us.

Second, I'm reminded God wants me to rejoice in what I *am* by the grace of God rather than rejoicing in the way God chooses to use me. My sanctification – the person I am becoming in Christ – is the crucial thing. Gifts are not primary. God is more interested in Jesus' character being

---

[19] Thank you, Jacob.

[20] I was the woman that invited 12 women over for Bible study and never offered even a glass of water. I mean, the Bible says the word IS bread and water. What do you mean, "Where's the tea and cookies?" It wouldn't have been so bad had I not lost track of time from pure zeal. Thankfully, none of those poor women were on the third floor listening in an open window.

developed in us, than how we are being used in ministry. Godly affections, Christ-likeness, these are the main.

And finally, J. I. Packer's words were instrumental in helping me to see my error:

> *Imagine, now a devoted and gifted Christian woman, whose ministry had been precious to her, finding that for quite a long period the Lord sidelines her so that her potential is not being used. What is going on? Is this spiritual failure? It is probably not spiritual failure at all, but a lesson in Christ's school of holiness. The Lord is reminding her that her life does not depend on finding that people need her. The prime source of her joy must always be the knowledge of God's love for her – the knowledge that though He did not need her, He has chosen to love her freely and gloriously so that she may have the eternal joy of fellowship with Him. Regarding her ministry, what matters is that she should be available to Him. Then He will decide when and how to put her to service again, and she should leave that with Him.*[21]

I did not have to imagine. That was me. I've learned I don't *fit* because I can do things. I *fit* because my Father loves me.

It's not equality we seek, but simply a place of service. "And the eye cannot say to the hand, 'I have no need of you'; nor again the head to the feet, 'I have no need of you'" (1 Cor. 12:21). In many denominations, 50% of the congregation is functionally ignored in order to keep women in their place. We need not limit all women's ministry out of fear that a woman will gain a following. Christian groupies happen with charismatically charged male personalities in the pulpit much more often than a rogue woman jockeying for a position that doesn't belong to her. Many congregations

---

[21] J. I. Packer, *Rediscovering Holiness: Know the Fulness of Life with God* (Grand Rapids: Baker Books, 2009). It should be noted that all 3 points above were pointed out to me through this precious resource.

have fallen because they followed a charming, affable male into a mess. If a woman teacher is worth her salt, she will be a woman who doesn't clamor for attention and a following of clones. She will humbly direct those she teaches to the elders and ministers in her church who have care over her soul and theirs. Her duty is to put her hand under chins and lift faces to Christ, to esteem her authorities and teach others to do likewise as a duty of disciple-making. I have no beef with parachurch ministries in which a woman teaches large groups of women. I do have a problem when she doesn't point those women back to the safe harbor of their husbands and their local church, encouraging them to remain under the authorities God has placed over them, both in the church and in the home. This is for our security, not our slavery.

Likewise, be Christlike

Do you want to be equal? Well, there is a way in which equality in the church is sanctioned and even promoted. It's in the *likewise.* Titus 2 begins with a charge to older men. As older women, it's a good idea to cultivate these older men attributes: "temperate, dignified, sensible, sound in faith, in love, in perseverance." In fact, Paul repeats a few of them for women.

> *Older women* ***likewise*** *are to be reverent in their behavior* [dignified], *not malicious gossips, nor enslaved to much wine* [temperate], *teaching what is good* [sound in faith], *so that they may encourage the young women to love their husbands, to love their children, to be sensible, pure, workers at home, kind, being subject to their own husbands, so that the word of God will not be dishonored.*[22] *Titus 2:3-5*

Did you see it? What is this *likewise?* Be a Christian, whether you are a man or a woman. Christ's character fits both. Keep in mind that God loves

[22] Emphasis and brackets mine.

you and is changing you into the image of His Son. Repent of any desire to serve God's church apart from His will for you. Believe that His love for you is better than any life you aspire to on your own.

These characteristics that we are to teach are the very character of Christ who dwells in us and in whom we move and have our being. They aren't male and female virtues. They are Christian virtues. Christly virtues. *Likewise* means "in like manner, in the same way, similarly." Are you looking for equality? Here it is. Like your brother in Christ, you get to image Jesus in every aspect of your life. Just be a Christian and, while you are at it, be a Christian girl. Stay in your lane.[23] We are all equally responsible to be like Christ. That's equality.

[23] I would say this to men as well. Stay in your lane. If you are elder material – be an elder. If you are deacon material – be a deacon. Do the work you are called to. Don't claim to be these and let your wife do the lion share of the work for you in the shadows. Go to work. House-husbanding while your wife is in the workforce is not man's calling. (There are good exceptions like age and health issues; otherwise, man up.)

Chapter 4

Woman to Woman

Older women… younger women…
Titus 2:3-4

Who's That Old Woman?

The *likewise* we saw earlier was directed to older women. Paul gives Titus a description (Titus 2:3) of virtues that are pertinent to our stage of life, in both the positive and the negative. Older women are to be role models in all their behavior and are called to teach and train younger women within the church.

I was the Women's Ministry Director at the First Baptist Church in our town. At the time, I was the young whipper-snapper. The church was a wealth of gray-haired ladies. They were cradle roll members. "I've been in this church since I was a baby, and I'll be here till I die." Most were absolutely delightful with only a few sprinkled with ornery and angst. I noticed they didn't mix much with the younger women. They had their own Sunday School class and their own mid-week Bible study led by the pastor at the church. They went to the traditional service, the early one with the organ and hymns. The younger women attended the contemporary service, the later one with the piano, guitar, and "worship songs." Their Bible studies were in homes during the week. Each year they were all invited to one event: the Ladies Tea. Even there, their tables were separated between the old and the young – unless we called it a Mother-Daughter Tea. This separation was both endearing and disheartening, and it was very difficult to change.

If I could revisit that time, I would work harder to bridge the gap between those groups. I confess those old women frightened me, but I can't for the life of me figure why. They were hidden resources that I failed to tap because of my own misperceptions. (Father, forgive me.) Older women are a treasure trove of wisdom, stories, fixes, and forgiveness. I learned that many of those women felt forgotten, as though they were of no use anymore. They were thought to be out of touch with today's struggles, yet they were experienced in God's ways. As a young woman, I assumed they were "through" with discipling and had decided to hunker down till Jesus came back. Actually, they didn't know what older women teaching younger women should look like. They had no pattern of discipleship to follow. And the younger women didn't believe these older women had anything to offer them. Now that I am older, maybe we can solve a few riddles regarding the older women in our pews.

We're Old and We Know Things

Older women want to be known and understood. We aren't all so feeble that we can't remember what it was like to have children hanging on us, messy houses, sport schedules, and menu boredom. Our children have not always been adults. Not as serious as many would surmise, given the chance, we can be quite fun. I'm a big fan of friendship and peers, iron sharpening iron, but it's tempting in peer relationships to allow sharing to become less sharpening and more commiserating. Not always, but sometimes. Older Christian women have learned how to cultivate the large fruits: hope, perseverance, forbearance, forgiveness, grace, contentment. We've lived long enough to discern between the temporal and the eternal, to see what's vital, what needs to be accepted and what needs to be rejected. Wisdom can be simple. It's good to remember that we aren't being trite, just abbreviated. We know things.

We would like young women to ask. We want to be useful and respected, but we don't want to be busybodies – at least most of us. We sometimes have a rough exterior, but we can be a little thin skinned. We get offended. Our time is not used in the way it once was. A common jest is, "Well, it's not like you *do* anything." Oh, but we do. It just looks different from the days when careers and children drew most of our attention. I'm not blind to the fact that many older people have stalled. They've "done their time and now it's your turn." Many think they've earned the right to leisure. Jesting doesn't encourage them toward usefulness, but invitation does. Granted, as we age, health declines and energy is a rare commodity. We still want to be drawn in to your young world. Many older women just need encouragement to find their place. There is an older woman in our church that creates beautiful birthday cards for our congregants. They are tailored to each person's likes. She also bakes our communion bread every Sunday and does it with joy. She is a true blessing. Another older woman makes authentic English tea for our fellowships. Her tea-brewing and jovial personality has won her access to the hearts of many of our younger women, well, that and the English accent. We need younger women to know that our lives didn't end the day our last child left the house. Older women want to be useful. Just ask us.

Older women need to be befriended. Recently, I was sitting in our worship service praying and, as clearly as if the Lord was sitting right next to me, I heard a still, small voice: "There's not one woman in this congregation that is not worth your knowing well." This is terrifying for someone like me who fears being known, but it's true. I'm committed to find a way to know the women in our congregation, even if it demands some humiliation and probably will mean a few missteps. Many of us just need a nudge, a tiny invitation into a young woman's world. In the vernacular of my high school years, we are longing to be invited to "the cool-kid table."

Older women are still growing up. About every five to seven years, I morph into somebody new. The change is so gradual that I don't wake up to it for a few years. I'm changing all the time. We all are. God is in the business of metamorphosis, conforming us to His will and image. An older woman's theology has become her life; her theology has left footprints to follow through some very difficult life circumstances. Many have battled through the death of parents and spouses and children, navigated terrible relationships and betrayals. We have contended with fluctuating hormones and suffered debilitating illnesses. We know what it's like to grieve over wayward children and to rejoice over their return. We know what it's like to come under God-given authority and to thrive even when that authority is tyrannical. Many of us have tamed our lusts and killed sin habits. Many of us have been broken and fixed and have labored in simple faith to remain steadfast in dark situations. We have learned and are still learning to navigate life. We've not lived perfectly, but we may be trusted because we understand the grace of God and have lived faithfully. We have tasted the fruit of repentance. We have learned to entrust ourselves to God and have experienced the pleasures of His right hand. We know things, and we want younger women to know things.

My husband and I gave financial advice to a young woman. Her husband was incarcerated. He was a brawler, violent and manipulative, but claiming to be a believer. She had a restraining order against him and was trying to take care of several children. My husband, a deacon, offered to help her order her finances so, in keeping with propriety, I stepped in to help. After our meeting, I walked her to the door. Emotions welled up. Her vulnerability was obvious. I said, "Did you know I haven't always been this person standing in front of you? At one point in my life, I was a lot like you." Her response made me laugh. "But your son is the pastor!" Yeah, in spite of my failures. The door was opened for me to dispel some very wrong assumptions. Older women haven't always been who they are in their old age. There's a whole life back there, sometimes a not so pretty one, and we are willing to share it.

Think about the women in your circle. Many came to Christ as children, many in their teens and twenties, some just yesterday. Age doesn't always mean wisdom. My mom and I came to Christ on the same day. I was in my late twenties; she in her late forties. She grew in her faith, but it wasn't a comet growth. It was a year after year, steady as she goes, through difficulties and questions, sort of growth. My Christian growth has been a little different. It looks like a very long roller coaster. Let's just say I've always had a bit more zeal in both the ups and the downs. A couple of days before my mom died, she asked, "Dennie, have I done enough? Will Jesus let me in?" Tears made their way down her cheeks. The shorter the time remaining, the more intense things can be. Fear had crept in. "Of course, mom. Your Lord is waiting for you. But no, you haven't done enough. None of us can ever do enough. Jesus has done it all, remember? You don't need to fear." She believed the gospel, but "Lord, help my unbelief" (Mark 9:24). Age doesn't mean we are immune to fear and doubt, but we aren't quitters either. We are still learning to overcome.

It doesn't matter our age, the Holy Spirit brings us to maturity from glory to glory, in His own time, in His own way. And though often it feels too late, God's timing is right. Only yesterday I sat with two women my age. One of them was quietly crying, lamenting that she had not raised her children well. She said, "The young women in our church are doing it all right. I watch them with their families, and I am so ashamed that I didn't know how to do that." She said out loud what many late blooming Christian women are thinking and feeling. It's not true that the young women in our church are doing *everything* right, but many of them are doing better than we did. We should rejoice in this. Older women can be extremely sensitive to their past failures. We preach to ourselves that we are and have always been maturing on God's timetable. We know we rarely get do-overs, but we can learn from the past, and many of us have. We know the truth now that we didn't know back then, and we are happy to share the way over, under, out, in, and especially through.

Who's That Young Woman?

I may not be young anymore, but I'm surrounded by young women. Here's what I think women my age should know about them.

First, young women are generally exhausted. When I say that, many older women want to cower in the corner because they think I'm advocating opening up their home like a daycare. You can come back and sit down. Frankly, when we get older, many of us don't have the energy to corral other people's children. Even the noise level is rough to deal with. We save our energy for our grandchildren, and that's about all we've got. If I may be blunt, we aren't called to be someone else's nanny. So be an encourager, older women. Help the young women around you to manage their stress. Teach them how NOT to be exhausted. Teach them to guard their time, set proper limits, get restorative sleep. Teach them wisdom. This does not mean reminding them that you had to wash clothes and dishes by hand, that you didn't have cell phones and computers, that two-car households were rare, and you had to rely on encyclopedias and libraries instead of Alexa, Siri, and Google. It was no tougher for you than it is now for them. Frankly, it's all those new resources and conveniences that have deceived all of us into believing we have more time in our schedules than we actually do. My advice to young women is to simplify as much as possible, to ignore trends that demand more of your time and produce little eternal fruit, and to genuinely ask God to point out excesses and underlying motives. Older women need to humble themselves and do what they can to give younger women relief. Remember, it wasn't very long ago that the dog destroyed the living room while you were away, the vacuum caught on fire, and the crayons in the dryer tie-dyed your daughter's best jeans. I'm sorry, that was me.

Younger women aren't stupid and you, older woman, are not their mom. I'm surrounded by brilliant younger women. More often than not, I stand back, mouth agape, wishing I'd known what they know. In my sphere, they are better mothers and better homemakers than I ever was. They have more Bible at their fingertips than at any other time in history and more resources available to them for spiritual growth than ever before. Many of them avail themselves of both. What they know though, often requires discipline they've yet to learn. Time and experience count for something. Even more, God sanctifies in the areas He chooses, when He chooses. Emotions run high, anxieties intensify, time constraints squeeze, and many young women feel like a zoo animal being watched and monitored. Masks abound. They snap an image of the one serene moment of their otherwise tumultuous day, put it on social media, and all of their peers think that is their life. "Is this what I am supposed to be like?" The hamster wheel starts turning and soon young women begin to believe that they aren't enough and, worse, other people now know it. Truthfully, no one is enough but Christ. He alone is sufficient, and young women have trouble grappling with that. They often have the answers, but not the wisdom to implement them. They need our grace, wisdom without condemnation, and our hospitality. Sometimes they just need a good night's sleep.

What can we do for them? Make a meal. Meals are not just for the sick. Invite them over so they have one less meal to prepare. Encourage play dates with other women and children. Take them groceries. Heck, take them shopping. Don't judge. Parenting is flippin' hard. Older women understand the power of consistency, perseverance, and joy. Pass it on to younger women. Show them and train them to let the Bible weigh in and direct every area of their lives. We must be "for" the young women around us, cheerleading and encouraging them. We want them to be better wives, better moms, more godly, more holy, more successful than we are.

Finally, young women often feel judged. Many of them have moms that have the freedom to say hard things – and sometimes over and over again. Some have moms-in-law that just want their baby boys taken care of and, by gosh, "she should do it the way I've always done it." Yuk.[24] We older women shouldn't react as though we've never seen a messy home or a messy kid. We have. It was our home and our kid. Judgment kills. Young women need our guidance and kindness more than our snark and criticism. They need us to look past the messes to their hearts, and to offer assistance where we can without a hint of the "you should'ves." Try to wait to be asked or in some way given permission, before you offer an opinion. My daughter thinks I'm the queen of the "have you considered..." plan. It's been my experience that many women don't push all the dominos down on

[24] To interject right here, if you are a mother-in-law, please strive to love your daughters-in-law. Be a good Naomi to your Ruths. Your sons are leaving and cleaving. YOU don't know how to be a good wife to your son. So be her friend as much as she will allow. And don't meddle.

the decisions they make, so I simply say, "Well, have you considered...?" It's a very non-threatening way to give an opinion. Although my friend Linda says when I use that phrase, she probably should brace for a rebuke. I'm still a big fan of asking the question. There's no judgment in just planting an alternative to the conundrum and allowing room for rumination. The crux is: offer wisdom without condemnation. Remember your own youth.

I'm certain I've not touched on everything in regard to the similarities and differences our age can cause. If you are young, repent of any fear or prejudice you might have against older women, and find an older woman to befriend. If you are older, repent of any fear or prejudice you might have against the younger women around you. Repent for not using the gifts God has given you to teach and train them, then find a younger woman to befriend – not as a project, but simply to love. Be humble. Care for one another. Love one another. I challenge you this Sunday, Christian woman, as you walk into your church building, to ask God to open your eyes to the women around you, old and young. There's not one woman in your congregation (including you) that is not worth knowing well.

Chapter 5

Reverent Living

Older women likewise are to be ***reverent*** *in their behavior…*
Titus 2:3a

It's fascinating to me that Paul doesn't simply say, "women likewise are to be reverent." Instead, he puts the emphasis on the *older* women. When I was younger, I tended to qualify this statement saying this could be defined as old in age *or* in spiritual maturity. I still believe that to be true, but now that I'm old with a little less hubris, I lean heavily toward this verse describing women older in age. It's a character trait that makes the wrinkles beautiful.

In the original language, *reverent* is only used in this verse in the Bible. We could rephrase this instruction to read "elder women are to suit the sacred." It is akin to the dignity that older men are commanded to exhibit.

Dignity, Always Dignity

If you've ever seen the musical *Singin' in the Rain*, you might sport a grin right here. At the beginning, Gene Kelly's character, Don Lockwood, is at a microphone narrating the origin story of his fame, which was anything but dignified. Yet he tells his audience his motto: "Dignity, always dignity." When Paul calls the older men to be dignified in Titus 2:2, he's calling for a much deeper character change that Mr. Lockwood had in mind. To be dignified is "to have formal reserve or a serious manner." It's "the quality or state of being worthy, honored, or esteemed." Thank you, Webster. The biblical use means to be venerable or reputable.

The kicker for this sort of dignity is not what it is, but where it comes from. Dignity is derived from something higher than ourselves, like a higher citizenship. As Christians, we understand that any dignity we have comes through our union with Jesus and our endowed citizenship in His kingdom. We are dignitaries in the kingdom of God, and our dignity is one that attracts and invites others to the One who gave us dignity in the first place.

Aristotle defined dignity as being the average between caring to please absolutely no one but self, and endeavoring at all costs to please everyone else.[25] One who has found the balance between narcissism and self-deprecation, between self-reliance and people-pleasing is dignified. In short, to be dignified is to live squarely between both extremes of pride. Decapitate the globe-head mentality ("the world revolves around me") and determine that the world also must not revolve around anyone else either. It only matters what God thinks of us. A dignified woman will care deeply about God's opinion and will live above reproach before an audience of One.

When I was a kid, getting attention wasn't a good thing. If I did well, the bar was raised even higher, and I was expected to hit or exceed that bar every time. Eventually, the bar would be unreachable. If I failed, which was often the case, the shame was unbearable. I always thought the best superpower would be invisibility. Though not a conscious decision, like a muted Walter Mitty, I zipped off in my mind to a "better reality," a place where I couldn't fail, where others always approved. It was an "I can't lose" world of my own. I lived there regularly. Every time I felt unloved, unwanted, or shamed, I walked through a doorway in my head, and I could live there for long blocks of time if needed.[26] One foot in the real world, one foot in mine (or so I thought). It was a fleshly, sinful attempt to survive shame and to

---

[25] Spiros Zodhiates, *The Complete Word Study Dictionary: New Testament* (Iowa: AMG Publishers, 1995), 1285.

[26] Well into my thirties, this behavior was finally given a name: dissociation. I'm free of it now, praise my Deliverer!

nurse some kind of dignity. I cared too deeply what people thought of me. And, well, I only thought of me.

When Christ brought me to Himself, you can imagine the internal upheaval He caused. God wrecked me in a good way. He began to dismantle my self-created world. In one particular time of prayer, I'm certain I heard the Holy Spirit speak to me, "I didn't save that fake girl you are parading around in your head. I saved you." I began telling myself *no* (with the help of the Holy Spirit) when my imagination was triggered. Gradually, *no* became *NO* and then it became "*You aren't the boss of me*" and then it became *never again.* God rocked my made-up world. Tremors. A bit of shaking here. A bit of shaking there. One day the earthquake hit and my fake world crumbled. I don't go there anymore. Gradually and finally, our Lord in His mercy rescued me from a world of my own making and gave me a little dignity, a little ballast, a little heavenly citizenship street cred. To be dignified is to know who we are in Christ and to put all the responsibility on Him to make us venerable and reputable, older men and women with godly stability and maturity. Which leads us back to repent and believe. A dignified person is one who might still have a pendulum swinging between the extremes, but like a metronome set on "presto," it ticks tightly and quickly and doesn't swing widely. It stays in the middle. Repent, believe, repent, believe, repent believe. Tick, tick, tick, tick, tick, tick. It's the heavenly rhythm of "Christ is enough and in him I am made complete."

I have some people in my life that personify dignity. They are steady beacons. They aren't boring; they are sure. They don't have to prove themselves, but they have many times proven themselves reputable. They are certain of their standing in Christ, dignitaries of the King who, by their humble dependence on Him for all things, show forth the glory and excellencies of Christ in the day-to-day, often mundane, duties of life. They look past themselves and their own circumstances to the joy set before them in Jesus Christ. Dignity brings ballast to the body of Christ as well. Dignified women are like ballerinas in the house of God – they're on point, balanced, steady and lovely.

There appears to be a subtle difference between dignity and reverence. I mean, why would Paul use two different words, one for men and one for women? Ironically, though all priests were men, this word for *reverence* is a priestly word meaning to be sacred, holy, consecrated to God. It carries the idea of being suitable and right. A reverent woman is someone whose behavior is fit for God's use. She's a holy woman whose behavior matches her godly innards.

Calling All Annas!

I call your attention to a woman who only gets three verses in Scripture, but they are doozies. She's a woman suited to sacredness, reverent in her behavior. Let me set the scene for you. Joseph and Mary brought their infant, Jesus, to the temple to present Him to the Lord[27] and to offer a sacrifice in accordance with the Law. The Holy Spirit reveals to Simeon that the baby is the Messiah. Simeon blesses them. Enter Anna, the providential eavesdropper.

> *And there was a prophetess, Anna the daughter of Phanuel, of the tribe of Asher. She was advanced in years and had lived with her husband seven years after her marriage, and then as a widow to the age of eighty-four. She never left the temple, serving night and day with fastings and prayers. At that very moment she came up and began giving thanks to God, and continued to speak of Him to all those who were looking for the redemption of Jerusalem. Luke 2:36-38*

Women in Israel typically got married around the age of thirteen.[28] It is possible that Anna was married at that age and was widowed at age twenty. For sixty-four years following, she remained a widow. We don't know for

---

[27] Please don't miss that! The Lord being presented to the Lord!

[28] This is an ever-lovin' mind blower! Imagine today's 13-year-old running a household!

certain, but she might have been childless. To be a widow was a guarantee of poverty. Even if she was left with a sizeable inheritance, which would have been unusual, her life would have to be characterized by prudence and frugality. The Scriptures state that she "did not depart from the temple." Because of her commitment to worshiping through prayer and fasting, it is very likely that the temple officiates gave Anna a small chamber in the outer court apartments in which to live. Though she held no office, her lifestyle or worship required nearness to the temple.

Anna's "sister" in the Old Testament is Hannah (1 Sam. 1), a woman very much like her. *Hannah*, in Hebrew, is *Anna*. Both were singled out for their practice of prayer and fasting. Both prophesied. Both seemed very comfortable in the temple. We don't know how old Hannah was, but we know she had been trying for quite some time to have a child. Both prayed concerning a child. Hannah for a son. Anna for the Son of God. Hannah gave her son to the Lord as an act of worship. Anna gave herself as an act of worship to the Son. Both believed. And both received.

What then does it look like to "suit the sacred?" What is a reverent woman? I see a few things in Anna that might direct us.

A reverent woman is a woman of the Word. We are told that Anna was a prophetess. A reverent woman's mind and conversation are occupied with the Word of God. Anna knew the Old Testament promises and banked on them. She looked to God for her own rescue as well as Israel's rescue. I would bet she habitually declared truth to other women – that's part of the role of a prophetess after all. A prophetess' words were to be for the edification, encouragement and consolation of the church (1 Cor. 14:3). Her heart was filled with God's word and it poured out into her relationships. When crisis bumps into you (or rolls over you), does the word of God spill out? Have you stored up a horde of promises to bank on in the tough seasons, or is your plan to tough it out on your own, or hope what you did last time will work this time? We must occupy ourselves with the word. "Let the word of Christ richly dwell within you, with all wisdom teaching and admonishing one another with psalms and hymns and spiritual songs, singing with thankfulness in your hearts to God" (Col. 3:16). "So faith comes from hearing, and hearing by the word of Christ" (Ro. 10:17). A reverent woman repents of a distracted heart and worldly pursuits, and becomes a woman who believes God's word. She drops anchor in the sea of God's promises.

A reverent woman is a worshiper. We find Anna in the temple worshiping with fasting and prayer. A reverent woman daily dwells in the presence of God and answers the call of God to worship each Sunday. We are to give every aspect and moment of our lives to the service of our Lord. This does not mean we isolate and forget our daily duties or neglect our families. No, I'm suggesting that the things we do throughout our day should be for the glory of God. Everything. "Whether, then, you eat or drink or whatever you do, do all to the glory of God" (1 Cor. 10:31).

Generally, I get up early, but I'm certainly not a morning person. I'm the person for whom Proverbs 27:14 was written. "He who blesses his friend with a loud voice early in the morning, it will be reckoned a curse to him." In my own words: A loud voice in the morning is a curse to the one who hears, not a blessing. I believe it. I seldom speak for at least a half hour in the morning unless I'm forced to by circumstance or visitor. That is, I don't talk out loud. Internally, there is a conversation running that started before my feet hit the floor. I quietly sing the Gloria Patri[29] to remind myself that my day is not my own. It lifts my chin and draws my gaze to God. It helps put intention into my day. I thank the Lord for waking me and helping me to get up and move. God stirs up a grateful attitude in me and reminds me that I have the pleasure of His company all day long. It helps me to work without grumbling. I remind myself that everything I have to do each day was a work prepared in advance by the One who created me. I tell God how I need His help and confess my sins and weaknesses. Then I receive His forgiveness and help, and I start to communicate with the rest of the world. Because of this ritual, which takes very little time and happens between my ears, I am better able to manage anything that is thrown at me throughout

[29] Gloria Patri: "Glory be to the Father, and to the Son, and to the Holy Ghost; as it was in the beginning, is now, and ever shall be, world without end. Amen. Amen."

my day, anything I didn't anticipate, and all those things that I did. My "to-do" list becomes more than just duty. It becomes a spiritual service of worship. The end of my day is similar. I'm a night owl. I wind down at night often with a book or a movie, but inevitably when my head hits the pillow, I have sung the Doxology[30] and I thank God for His preservation and for upholding me. I rejoice in the mercies of the day, thanking Him that His goodness has chased me down once again.

> *I will extol You, my God, O King, and I will bless Your name forever and ever. Every day I will bless you, and I will praise Your name forever and ever. Great is the LORD, and highly to be praised, and His greatness is unsearchable. One generation shall praise Your works to another, and shall declare Your mighty acts. On the glorious splendor of Your majesty and on Your wonderful works, I will meditate. Men shall speak of the power of Your awesome acts, and I will tell of Your greatness. They shall eagerly utter the memory of Your abundant goodness and will shout joyfully of Your righteousness. Psalm 145:1-7*

> *Therefore, since we receive a kingdom which cannot be shaken, let us show gratitude, by which we may offer to God an acceptable service with reverence and awe; for our God is a consuming fire. Hebrews 12:28-29*

For me, I think service that works throughout the day, that does the dishes and makes the bed and pays the bills and sweeps the floors, that kind of worship finds its root in Psalm 73:25. "Whom have I in heaven *but You?* And besides You, I desire nothing on earth." In the words of songwriter and singer Rich Mullins, God is our "one thing." Worship is single-hearted focus on the One who owns us.

---

[30] Doxology: "Praise God from whom all blessing flow; Praise Him all creatures here below; Praise Him above, ye heav'nly host; Praise Father, Son, and Holy Ghost."

> *Save me from those things that might distract me. Please take them away and purify my heart. I don't want to lose the eternal for the things that are passing 'cause what will I have when the world is gone if it isn't for the love that goes on and on with my one thing. You're my one thing.*[31]

I think Anna understood that. God had become her one thing.

A reverent woman is a warrior. Anymore, it seems like every crime show on television has a woman detective who can solve a case in a day or two, rough up the perps, and humiliate her male partner, all with tight black plants, a blouse one size too small, and heels. This is not the kind of woman-warrior God esteems. No, the marks of a warrior in God's kingdom are calloused knees and a sore throat. Anna prayed for the redemption of Israel and saw her answer in the face of Jesus that day in the temple. While the rest of the world went about their business, she prayed and the kingdom came.

I'll give you an example of this from one of the reverent women in my life. Her name was Rose. I was about thirty. She was about fifty. We were in a small Baptist church in Oklahoma. Every Sunday I struggled *not* to watch her. I felt like a spiritual stalker. She wore her long, bright red hair in a bun. It was never smooth. It was always a bit disheveled and seemed sort of tilted, a heavy leaning tower of hair. She was unpretentious. She sang beautifully and loud, hands raised in worship, face lifted like she could see God through the ceiling. During the altar call, she would go up to the kneeling benches. There she would kneel to pray, not silently, but quietly. I would steal to the front and kneel right beside her and listen to her pray. Internally, I would echo, "What she said, Lord." Unaware, Rose taught me to pray.[32] She understood that from song to supplication, the war was on, and she was a fighter, instant and persevering in prayer. "Moreover, as for me,

---

[31] James Bryan Smith, *An Arrow Point to Heaven: Rich Mullins – His Life and Legacy* (Nashville: Broadman and Holdman, 2000), 126-127.

[32] Thank you, Rose, for the tutorial. You were a reverent woman indeed.

far be it from me that I should sin against the Lord by ceasing to pray for you, and I will instruct you in the good and the right way" (1 Sam. 12:23).

Prayerlessness and ingratitude are silent assassins. To refuse to pray is to pridefully announce that we have no need of God's help. We're handling life just fine. And ingratitude gives prayerlessness an amen. It says what God has given is not enough. These are such insults to our God. These two assassins see no need for worship. They kill reverence. Many of us rather than fight *to* pray, lapse into self-sufficiency. Sometimes it truly is a battle just to pray. But it's amazing, isn't it, when we are in crisis, how quick we holler to our Lord for help? Being a reverent woman means we learn to pray, earnestly and consistently, in quiet and in crisis. John Calvin said, "To know God as the Master and Bestower of all good things, who invites us to request them of Him, and still not go to Him and ask of Him – this would be of as little profit as for a man to neglect a treasure, buried and hidden in the earth, after it had been pointed out to him."[33] We must repent of our prayerlessness if we desire to be reverent women. To be a warrior is to be aware of our own impotence and our great need for God's intervention in even the little things. Imagine knowing exactly where the treasure is buried, knowing that the answer to your every need is in a box in the ground, but refusing to grab a shovel. We have a standing invitation from our Maker to come boldly before His throne, to ask for the answer to every need, to converse with Him about every thought, every anxiety, every joy, to receive from Him all that we need for His glory and our joy. We only have to ask. Believe and be brave. Be a warrior. And it wouldn't hurt to simply pray for the pleasure of His company.

One more thing concerning older women and the privilege of prayer – if you are looking for a place of ministry in the body of Christ, a place to be of use, prayer is not a lesser place of service. It is *the* service. It is priestly and royal. For a number of years, my mom was paralyzed from the neck down, suffering from an extremely rare disease. She was completely dependent upon others for all of those things that we take for granted: eating, drinking,

[33] John Calvin, *Institutes of the Christian Religion* (Grand Rapids: William B. Eerdmanns Publishing, 1979), 850.

bathing, teeth brushing, hair washing. One evening she was lamenting that she was a burden to so many people. "Why would God let this happen? I can't serve Him at all like this." Had I been in her place, I have no doubt I would have believed the same. But I said to her, "Mom, pray for me. Pray for us. God has given you the highest calling: pray." And she did. Listen to God's words to the gray-haired heads: "Now she who is a widow indeed and who has been left alone, has fixed her hope on God and continues in entreaties and prayers night and day. But she who gives herself to wanton pleasure is dead even while she lives" (1 Tim. 5:5-6). I bet many of you didn't even know that was in the Bible. This kind of prayer is learned *before* we become widows. Younger women should be cultivating a life of prayer now. It's not too late if you are already old. Take up your position in the body of Christ like my mom did. Remember you have a strategic role to play. Set your hope on God and pray with all of His might. Be the woman who skids into heaven on her knees.

A reverent woman is an expectant woman. Anna set her face toward the Lord and His promises. She waited on Him with full assurance of faith. She might have even heard others mocking her and saying, "Where is the promise of His coming? For ever since the fathers fell asleep, all continues just as it was from the beginning of creation" (2 Pet. 3:4). But she was steadfast in her faith and her hope was rewarded. She saw her redemption in the face of the tiny newborn Christ. We find our hope in the resurrected and reigning Christ. "...to whom God willed to make known what is the riches of the glory of this mystery among the Gentiles, which is Christ in you, the hope of glory" (Col. 1:27). Our hope is found in the very presence of Christ in us, in the church and in each of us by His Spirit. A reverent woman is called to live her life in full assurance of faith, being filled with the Holy Spirit and expecting nothing less than for God's will to be accomplished in every aspect of her life and her world. We are to have a high view of God's rule over us. His love and sovereignty should fly like a banner over us as we wait expectantly for His will to be accomplished, His good, pleasing and perfect will. Like Anna, we are to give thanks to God and speak of Him to everyone who is waiting for His redemption. If you need it, I give you permission to be gushy about your God. Proclaim His goodness.

Anna's (and Hannah's) name means *grace*. I think she may have determined that all of her life was indeed grace. In spite of loss at a very young age, she must have been lavished with the grace of God. In some mysterious way, I think she must have grasped a truth way beyond her years, one Paul stated in Ephesians 1:7-12:

> *In Him we have redemption through His blood, the forgiveness of our trespasses, according to the riches of His grace which He lavished on us. In all wisdom and insight He made known to us the mystery of His will, according to His kind intention which He purposed in Him with a view to an administration suitable to the fullness of the times, that is, the summing up of all things in Christ, things in the heavens and things on the earth. In Him also we have obtained an inheritance, having been predestined according to His purpose who works all things after the counsel of His will, to the end that we who were the first to hope in Christ would be to the praise of His glory.*

Though not prominently placed in those three little verses concerning Anna, I believe we can add one more attribute to the model of a reverent woman.

A reverent woman fears God. "Charm is deceitful and beauty is vain, *but* a woman who fears the LORD, she shall be praised" (Prov. 31:30). And "the fear of the LORD is to hate evil; Pride and arrogance and the evil way and the perverted mouth, I hate" (Prov. 8:13). To be reverent is to fear the Lord and hate what He hates. One of the best definitions I've ever come upon concerning the fear of God is this: A person who fears the Lord wisely sides with God in everything. This is important for Christian women, old and young.

To make this clear, let me give you an example of what fear of the Lord isn't. When I was young, my father could be a little scary. He was a military man, a stickler for excellence and promptness. He seldom handed out second chances. I quickly learned to view everything in my life on a pass/fail basis. When I was a child, what I remember most about my dad was his shoes, black polished with slender laces, so polished I could see my reflection in them. I don't remember his face back then. I never raised my head to look at his face. Head down. Shoes. Every childlike mistake felt like a mortal sin. I feared him and he taught me to fear just about everything.[34]

But this is not the kind of fear God is calling us to. Godly fear does not create cowards. Psalm 103:13-14 reads, "Just as a father has compassion on *his* children, so the LORD has compassion on those who fear Him. For He Himself knows our frame; He is mindful that we are *but* dust." Godly fathers are compassionate fathers. God our Father is compassionate to those who fear Him.

> *For we do not have a high priest who cannot sympathize with our weaknesses, but One who has been tempted in all things as we are, yet without sin. Therefore let us draw near with confidence to the throne of grace, so that we may receive mercy and find grace to help in time of need. Hebrews 4:15-16*

Because Christ has gone before us, we now have safe passage into the throne room of God. Christ has made a way into God's presence through the veil of His own flesh, making a way for us to come boldly, head held up, speaking our mind, into the holy of holies. Not arrogantly, yet full of assurance that we are loved, accepted, and received. God wants us to see His face, not His shoes. Proverbs tells us "the fear of the LORD is a fountain of life, that one may avoid the snares of death" (14:27) and that "the fear of the LORD *leads* to life, so that one may sleep satisfied, untouched by evil." Scandalously marvelous, isn't it? Could you use a "satisfied" night's sleep? Would you like evil to be unable to touch you? Fear the Lord.

---

[34] I say these things not with anger or disdain, but with great love for my father. Knowing his history, I can forgive him. After all, God forgave him, loves him, and I love him.

A right fear of the Lord removes condemnation, judgment, and shame and frees us to serve Him with joy. A reverent woman – a wise woman – takes God's side in everything and can't stand His displeasure because she loves Him and hates what He hates. This is a woman who fears the Lord.

Finally, to the younger women and peers of reverent women: Reverent women should be revered. "You shall rise up before the gray-headed and honor the aged, and you shall revere your God; I am the LORD" (Lev. 19:32). When we recognize reverence in women – and we certainly should in older, mature Christian women – we are to honor them. To honor her is to fear God.

Chapter 6

Devil of an Opportunity

Older women likewise are to be reverent in their behavior,
not malicious gossips...
Titus 2:3

If you've ever been the victim of slander, you know the aftermath of bewilderment and hurt it leaves behind. I don't know about you, but just being misunderstood is often enough to put my head under the covers. To be publicly labeled something you are not is a betrayal that can fracture a soul. Victims of slander often respond in one of two ways: they attempt to vindicate themselves and restore their sullied name or they retreat into isolation and hope it will eventually all be forgotten. I'm guilty of opting for the first in my thoughts and the latter in my deeds. As a result, shame has had its way with me far too often.

Side With God

Remember, within the definition of *reverence* is the idea of siding with God over the enemy and over others. To be a malicious gossip or slanderer is to side with God's enemies. It's interesting that, for the most part, this sin plagues women more than men. We women have mastered the art of redefining gossip into prayer requests and feigning compassion when we just want to be in the know. Slander is a subtle little imp. It opposes the purposes of God. When we speak against someone, especially a brother or sister in Christ, we are taking the enemy's side.

A slanderer is a false witness, an accuser, who divides people without reason. In the Bible, the word is translated *diabolos*. Think *diabolical*. This word is used as Satan's name about 38 times in Scripture. Akin to it is the word *blasphemy*, which is injurious speech or vilification. We find this word used in Colossians 3:8. "But now you also, put them all aside: anger, wrath, malice, slander (*blasphemia*), and abusive speech from your mouth."

God is calling us to side with Him in all aspects of speech – to stand against sin, to speak the truth in love, and to guard against impure thoughts and motives because out of the abundance of the heart, the mouth speaks (cf. Luke 6:45). The natural question is how? And the first step is to own any impure thoughts and words before God. If we struggle with this (and all of us do), avoiding makes it worse. We are to repent of any known sin in our speech and, beholding Christ through His word, we put off sin and put on Christ. Repent, believe, and obey. This isn't a trite thing. I understand the battle is real and sometimes very difficult, but we are to take God seriously in regard to godly thoughts and speech. The Bible *says* so.

I have some close friends who, by virtue of their love for me, are privy to my frustrations. They are grace givers and great listeners. I also have a relationship that, if I may use Oklahoma speak, annoys the tar out of me. Unfortunately for my close friends, their ears have heard more than my mouth should have said. Maybe you don't have to repent as often as I do, but just this week I vented about that one relationship and realized I was pushing the slander envelope. It's not slander if it's true, right? The Holy Spirit called me out on my motive. Even if it's true, I can't recall God ever saying, "Dennie, you just need to vent your anger toward silly 'ole so-and-so with your buddies and that will produce godliness and peace. Just let it out!" Said God never! There are times when we truly have a deep concern for someone. In the aforementioned example, the woman was hurting others I love. I realized I needed to go to her directly. My over-sharing with my friends came out of hurt and fear. We just want someone else to help carry the load. I sympathize, but as a wise person once said, "Stop it."

The Art of Tattling

I'm a natural born tattler. If you don't believe me, just look back at the last paragraph. I even tattle on myself. I like rules. I respect them. As a kid, if I did not outright tattletale, I would see to it that my brothers were found out. (Sorry bros.) As I've grown up, physically and in my faith, I've refined the art of tattling to God. He is my first call when I am offended, slighted, mistreated, or just plain ticked off. I can't count how many times I have said to our heavenly Father. "Did You see that? Did You hear what they said?" It's true. Most of the time, the sin gets resolved quickly in my heart. Why? Because God always points out my own sin first. I'm called to cover a multitude of sins by others, look at my own sin, repent, and shut the heck up. Tattling to God is usually rewarded with a much-appreciated divine kick in the pants. I'm okay with it. It keeps me from choosing the "phone a friend" option.

I bring up tattling because sometimes it's necessary to tattle to a human. We may have to share information that is true about someone. True words can damage a person's reputation, but that doesn't mean they shouldn't be said. Real sins sometimes have to be brought into the light for the protection of others. For instance, it's not slanderous to "out" someone who is a proven abuser or drug user – but we should out them to the proper people, not just for the sake of humiliating them or easing our own anger or distress. Rather, we do it out of love, for their good and for their salvation. We must be certain of the facts. Hearsay is slander and certainly doesn't warrant a serious accusation.

I recently found myself in a conundrum between keeping a confidence with one of my dearest friends, and ratting out some really bad behavior on the part of her son who attended my church. It wasn't an easy place to live. I prayed and reasoned, "Am I slandering, gossiping, or speaking the truth?" "Am I protecting an abuser and putting other lives in jeopardy?" "What will this do to my friend?" Turns out the accusation was true and the elders in my church needed to step in. What I had to say was just more evidence of an already exposed sin. What my friend had shared with me, my elders already knew. The truth has to win out. God was gracious in this situation. The person that tattled first to our church leadership just happened to be an eyewitness in law enforcement. These kinds of sins can't stay hidden. "Behold, you have sinned against the LORD, and be sure your sin will find you out" (Num. 32:23). Thankfully, our elders are true elders and the situation was rightly dealt with.

I'm hounding this topic because another big trend in some mainline churches is a clamp on *any* sharing of information. Remember, slander is destructive. But all sharing is not gossip, or what the Bible defines as "secret slandering" (2 Cor. 12:20). I'm aware of a few pastors who, in order to keep guard over their own below-reproach reputations, accused the majority of their own congregations of gossip and slander, and then laid down hard and fast rules about what could be shared with whom. By the time the rules were in place, everyone was forbidden to talk personally about anything, unless of course it was with the pastor, and he gave himself the liberty to share whatever he deemed prudent, or whatever put himself in the best light. What about real grievances? "Gossip." What about problems with a spouse, a family member, a friend? "Gossip." What if the pastor is in gross sin? "Gossip." "Slander." In some of these churches, to follow the guidelines of Matthew 18:15-17 was to be a slanderer. Granted, this scenario is rare, but it is real. We need to define things biblically and follow the principles set down in Scripture to keep the leaders *as well as* the members of the church accountable to God and to one another.

Let's review. Slander is *untrue* information about others. All true information doesn't need to be shared. Love really does cover a multitude of sins. Friends don't let friends slander friends. Truth-telling that will injure a person's reputation is still sometimes necessary if the sin and abuse are confirmed and documented. This is done to save the sinner from destruction and to save those around him (or her) from the sin. This is also done discreetly and to the proper authorities, whether spiritual or civil.

Wicked Speak

I've compiled a list of ways the Bible describes wicked or perverse speech. As reverent elder women, we want to have sound speech in every area, so let me focus your gaze on the other little foxes in the vineyard. Set your sight and take aim at them, but try not to shoot the messenger. Here they are: maligning others, malicious gossip, busybodies, troublesome meddlers,[35] unwholesome words,[36] filthiness,[37] silly talk,[38] coarse jesting,[39] lying, slander, abusive speech, careless words, swearing oaths and not keeping them, worldly and empty chatter (which can often lead to tall tales), insulting, biting and devouring, grumbling and disputing, evil speech and deceit, hasty words, too many words, and arrogant and boastful words. I doubt this is a comprehensive list. We worldlings are a wily lot.

Our biggest target in that list ought to be a lying tongue. "There are six things which the LORD hates, yes, seven which are an abomination to Him: Haughty eyes, *a lying tongue,* and hands that shed innocent blood, a heart that devises wicked plans, feet that run rapidly to evil, *a false witness who utters lies,* and one who spreads strife among brothers" (Prov. 6:16-19). Oh. My. No wonder the psalmist prays, "Deliver my soul, O LORD, from lying lips, from a deceitful tongue" (Ps. 120:2). I recently finished reading a vastly needed book (for any and all) by Peter J. Leithart. In it he masterfully walks through the Ten Words or Ten Commandments. In his chapter

---

[35] This is someone who enjoys overseeing the affairs of other people. A butter-inner. This could be someone who gives unnecessary or even wrong advice – sometimes just to stir the pot or slap the beehive. Pick your colloquialism.

[36] Rotten and unfit for use words – cursing, vile language. The idea is words that leave a putrid odor.

[37] Shameful, obscene, crude speech

[38] Foolishness or buffoonery – I wonder if this could be speech that taunts and treats others like fools or joking to the point of embarrassing someone else. Just a thought.

[39] God is not a sad sack. He isn't opposed to humor. Just look up *laughter* in the Bible. But this could mean "low humor." Some definitions given are scurrility (vilifying, indecent or vulgar remarks), ribaldry (mocking, abusive, irreverent remarks) and low jesting.

concerning the ninth word, "Thou shalt not bear false witness," Dr. Leithart stresses truth-telling in a compelling way.

> *The Ninth Word parallels the Fourth, the Sabbath command. On the Lord's Day, we confess the Truth that is Jesus Christ, hear the truth from Scripture and sermon, sing the truth. The liturgy trains us in truth-telling. It forms the church as a truth-living people, sons of the Father through the eternal Son. Truth-telling isn't necessarily 'nice.' We learn to be truth-tellers when we learn to see clearly and when we break the habit of covering our cowardice with the pious excuse of 'love.' Immediately after Yahweh forbids Israelites to hate their countrymen (Lev. 19:17) and immediately before he tells them to 'love your neighbor as yourself (Lev. 19:17-18 NASB), he tells them to "reprove your neighbor" (Lev. 19:17 NASB). Prophets like Nathan (2 Sam. 12) and Elijah (1 Kings 17-19) weren't nice. They really performed the cliché: they spoke truth to power. And their blistering words carried divine power, to pluck up and plant, to demolish and build (cf. Jer. 1:10). Truthful correction is an expression of love, not hate. If you tell the truth, you will create conflict, and then you are called to be a peacemaker. But true peace can be won only if the truth shatters the false peace of the lie... Truthful speech is an act of love, and we are to love enemies as well as friends. In all normal circumstances, we speak truth to and about our enemies, refusing to minimize their virtues or exaggerate their faults.*[40]

All wicked speech seems to have a hint of deceit in it somewhere. All good speech boils down to truth-telling, doesn't it? God is calling us to speak truth because He is truth. That same truth sanctifies us and edifies others.

---

[40] Peter J. Leithart, *The Ten Commandments: a Guide to the Perfect Law of Liberty* (Washington: Lexham Press, 2020), 108-110.

God Speak

What is the origin of our words? Jesus told us:

> *You brood of vipers, how can you, being evil, speak what is good? For the mouth speaks out of that which fills the heart. The good man brings out of his good treasure what is good; and the evil man brings out of his evil treasure what is evil. But I tell you that every careless word that people speak, they shall give an accounting for it in the day of judgment. For by your words you will be justified, and by your words you will be condemned. Matthew 12:34-37*

> *It is not what enters into the mouth that defiles the man, but what proceeds out of the mouth, this defiles the man. Matthew 15:11*

Considering these truths, we are constrained then by a new heart, a completely renovated one by the Holy Spirit. This happens when we are born again. We aren't born again *because* we repent and believe. It's because we have a new heart that we are able to repent and believe. Unbelievers are most certainly dead in their trespasses and sins. God, in His mystery and grace, changes our hearts by removing the old heart of stone, and giving us a soft heart, one of flesh, one that is alive and capable of faith and obedience. He even gives us the faith to believe. We are indeed saved by grace through faith (see Eph. 2:1-10). The prerequisite for any and all change in our thoughts, character, or attitudes must be a true salvation begun by a heart transplant. That understood, all change comes by repentance and faith progressively throughout our Christian life in unity with Christ. It's an "already-not-yet" life that we live.

If we want godly speech, and as Christians we certainly do, then the next step is the transformation of our thoughts. "And do not be conformed to this world, but be transformed by the renewing of your mind, so that you may prove what the will of God is, that which is good and acceptable and perfect" (Ro. 12:2). We put off all of those sinful ways of speaking by confession and repentance, and true repentance puts on the good speech of Christ by faith. I'm assuming we are reading the word and believing it.

> *Let the word of Christ richly dwell within you... Colossians 3:16*

> *For the word of God is living and active and sharper than any two-edged sword, and piercing as far as the division of soul and spirit, of both joints and marrow, and able to judge the thoughts and intentions of the heart. Hebrews 4:12*

> *Like newborn babies, long for the pure milk of the word, so that by it you may grow in respect to salvation, if you have tasted the kindness of the Lord. 1 Peter 2:2-3*

The Proverbs give us examples of righteous speech and its benefits.

Speak with few words. The Proverbs warn us that too many words make transgression unavoidable. Think about the last time you tried to cover your proverbial behind with a stream of words. Restrained words (as well as silence) prove wisdom. My sons have made this an art. When they speak, their words are thoughtful and weighted. They don't get caught up in their own rhetoric. They are young, still in their thirties, and yet marked by wisdom. My dad was a pro at this, but not necessarily a wise man. We can be considered prudent simply by knowing when to speak and when to keep silent. He often quoted Abe Lincoln, "It's better to remain silent and be thought a fool than to speak and to remove all doubt."

Speak wisely. Our speech is to be thoughtful and wise. Wise speech heals; rash speech injures. We are to set guards over our mouths for our own protection. A guarded mouth guards a soul from trouble and preserves life. A man without a mouthguard comes to ruin.

Speak gently. We answer others with gentle words. This turns away wrath. Harsh words stir up anger. Have a soothing tongue – it's a tree of life.

Speak fit words. Let your words be timely. There is joy in an apt answer and delight in a timely word. God says a word spoken in the right circumstances is lovely. Consider before speaking. It's so much better to ponder your response than to wish you could have your words back. One benefit to aging is our brains slow down. (Who knew that could be a good thing?) We get ourselves into less trouble because it takes us longer to process a sentence.

Speak rightly. Righteous speech is speech seasoned with truth and wisdom. It's "a delight to those in authority" and the Bible says that he who speaks right is loved. Akin to that is persuasive speech which comes from a wise heart instructing the mouth. Be pleasant, knowledgeable (but not pompous), and reprove with your words, but consider the frame of the one in front of you. Pay attention to 1 Thessalonians 5:14: "We urge you, brethren, admonish the unruly, encourage the fainthearted, help the weak, be patient with everyone." Don't keep your counsel button on "admonish." Be aware of the person you're talking with. And remember, fools hate wisdom. Don't let foolish women draw you into fruitless arguments.

Speak weighty words. A listener is a beautiful thing. Keep confidences and be kind and prudent, using loving, unifying words. Weigh your words carefully, giving thought to your replies. It's the careless words that are judged.

Speak honestly. Speak truth to one another because we are members of one another, and because we have laid aside the old self and have put on the new.

Speak gratefully. Let your words represent a truly thankful heart. It's just proper. Give grace to those who hear by using edifying words according to the hearer's need. Words that flow from a heart of gratitude always edify.

Your words are important.[41]

I know. It's overwhelming. So let me encourage you. James 3 is a brief teaching on the tongue. Though frightfully convicting, it brings out some very gracious truth. "For we all stumble in many ways. If anyone does not stumble in what he says, he is a perfect man, able to bridle the whole body as well" (James 3:2). Whew! What a relief! I'm not the only one. James uses examples to show us the importance of getting our mouths under control. Ships are huge, but can be directed by a small rudder. If we get the tongue (a very small rudder) under control, we can get the whole body to do what it's supposed to do. The tongue can destroy indiscriminately. An entire forest can be set aflame by one little campfire mismanaged. Just ask the bear.[42] Uncontrolled tongues can wreak havoc in relationships. Though the tongue is untamable, it is controllable by the Holy Spirit and our willing submission to His will, so we must take advantage of this divine resource, believing that, as He promised, He will teach us what to say.

But I Was Slandered

Now that the rabbit trail, albeit a profitable one, has ended, let's go back to dealing with malicious gossips and slanderers from another perspective. What do we do when *we* are the slandered ones? What's the proper response when we are the subject of gossip? I'm no stranger to either side of the coin. To slander is to take the side of the enemy, but to be slandered is to have Christ on our side.

I've already alluded to the fact that one of my greatest hates is to be misunderstood. I want people to know me, and I despise being thought to be something other than I truly am. Doesn't everyone? I went through a

---

[41] For the treasure hunt and proof that I am not kidding: Proverbs 10:19, 11:12, 12:18, 13:3, 15:1-2, 15:28, 16:13, 16:23-24, 17:27-28, 18:13, 20:15, 20:19, 21:23, 23:9, 31:26, Galatians 5:14-15, Matthew 12:36, Ephesians 4:25, 4:29, 5:4, Colossians 3:18-19.

[42] I refer here to the venerable "Smokey the Bear," that hat wearing, cigarette stomping *ursus americanus.*

season several years back when I was branded with some awful adjectives. Granted, sometimes there is an element of truth in words people sling at us. My heart was ruptured, emotions all over the place, and I couldn't discern my sin from the sins of others. God alone had the right record. Not all, but much of what was said about me during that season simply was not true. I had been slandered. What ratcheted the pain even more was that I couldn't find a way to clean up the misunderstanding. Even worse was the fact that much of the slander came from people that I dearly love. Graciously, God began to yank on prideful roots of fear and self- pity, and to toughen up the cowardly heart I wore on my sleeve. He reminded me (and I continue to remind myself) that I am in good company. Jesus certainly knows what it feels like to be misunderstood and have His character muddied with lies. Pride always wants to set the record straight. I was never able to do that. Though I've tried to be at peace with everyone involved, forgiving and making attempts at reconciliation, there are still people I love and miss who remain in the slandering camp while I remain misjudged. Jesus would have us persevere through situations like this. It helps to realize it is not our own reputation that is at stake. Jesus is perfectly capable of defending Himself. It's His name and His glory that are tantamount, not the whispers about us and our measly reputations.

Responding Rightly

From God's word brought to bear on my own experience, I have learned to better navigate through these particular offenses. One way is to talk to God first, not the slanderer. Charles Spurgeon is quoted as saying, "When the devil opens his mouth in slander it gives me an opportunity to ram the sword of truth down his throat." That'll do it, right? But he also said,

> *It is a fine thing, when you are slandered, not to hear it. And it is a better thing to never reply to it. I have always tried to possess one deaf ear and one blind eye – and I believe that the deaf ear is the better ear and the blind eye by far the more*

> *useful of the two. Do not remember the injury that is done to you, try to forget it and pass it over. Do not go about the world determined to grasp every red-hot iron that any fool holds out before you. Let it alone! It will be for your own good and for God's glory to be very patient under the slander of the wicked.*[43]

Peter reminds us of Jesus' response to revilers and encourages us:

> *For you have been called for this purpose, since Christ also suffered for you, leaving you an example for you to follow in His steps, WHO COMMITTED NO SIN, NOR WAS ANY DECEIT FOUND IN HIS MOUTH; and while being reviled, He did not revile in return; while suffering He uttered no threats, but kept entrusting Himself to Him who judges righteously. 1 Peter 2:21-23*

> *Beloved, do not be surprised at the fiery ordeal among you; but to the degree that you share the sufferings of Christ, keep on rejoicing so that also at the revelation of His glory you may rejoice with exultation. If you are reviled for the name of Christ, you are blessed, because the Spirit of glory and of God rests on you. Make sure that none of you suffers as a murderer, or thief, or evildoer, or a troublesome meddler; but if anyone suffers as a Christian, he is not to be ashamed but is to glorify God in this name. 1 Peter 4:12-16*

Following Christ's example is never a bad thing. The second option is Paul's example: entreat.

> *To this present hour we are both hungry and thirsty, and are poorly clothed, and are roughly treated, and are homeless; and*

---

[43] Charles Haddon Spurgeon, *Expositions by C. H. Spurgeon – Psalm 38.*

> *we toil, working with our own hands; when we are reviled, we bless; when we are persecuted, we endure; when we are slandered, we try to conciliate* [entreat]*; we have become as the scum of the world, the dregs of all things, even until now. 1 Corinthians 4:11-13*

The word *conciliate* is a form of the word used to describe the Holy Spirit as our Comforter. It means "to call someone to our side or to come alongside." The Holy Spirit appeals to us and comes alongside us, urging us to walk as Christ walked. Like the Holy Spirit, we can appeal to someone to see our side of things, to walk next to us in love. This certainly doesn't mean compromising the truth. We are also never guaranteed the relationship will be restored or the slander will stop. But when we take this option, we can say we have done everything to be at peace with all men. We can appeal to others with the truth, but we can't force them to believe us.

How do you know which is the wisest way to respond? The Holy Spirit will call us to His side and reveal to us the best way to handle the situation. This, along with some strong, godly church elders is a great plan for discerning what to do. Stay connected to a church and remain under its authority, seek godly counsel, and trust the Lord to lead you by the Spirit and through His people into righteousness. The bottom line? When the coin is flipped and you are slandered or misunderstood, have one deaf ear, one blind eye, and a reconciling tongue. When the coin is flipped again and you are tempted to slander someone, have a swollen tongue and a gracious, forgiving heart. Remember Who is on your side and Whose side you are on. And be faithful.

Chapter 7

Safe and Sound

> *Older women likewise are to be reverent in their behavior, not malicious gossips nor enslaved to much wine, **teaching what is good...***
>
> *Titus 2:3*

***Kalodidaskalos*. I've been** trying today to learn how to pronounce that: ka-lo-de-da-ska-los. After the first syllable, you add la-de-da and ska-los. In my head, I'm saying it to the tune of ta-ra-ra-boom-de-a. Anyway, *kalodidaskalos* is the transliteration for the Greek word for *teachers of good things* or *teachers of goodness,* our next elder woman virtue.[44]

Paul gives us a sampling of the good we are to teach here in Titus, but this is of course not *all* the good we are to teach. Certainly, these are a priority for women. Why are we to teach them? I find a two-fold reason:

1. Younger women need training (2:4).
2. The word of God must be honored (2:5).

This, in my opinion, hearkens back to Titus 2:2 and the admonition to the older men to be sound in faith, in love, and in perseverance. We don't get a pass. We are to be these things as well. Titus, in his instruction to those called to be elders (1:9), calls men to be sound in doctrine. The Bible is our

[44] I know I skipped the admonition to not be enslaved to much wine. We will return to it later.

main source for sound doctrine. The word: read, preached, heard. Our older men (especially our own husbands and the church elders charged with care over us) are to not only teach younger men, but the other fifty percent of the congregation – women. Faith, love, perseverance, and doctrine are all part of the good we are to teach. It looks different when we women do it, but I believe it is our responsibility to our younger sisters in Christ. Let's flesh this out a little by backing up to what is *sound*.

Sound Doctrine

We often use the expression "safe and sound." To be *sound* is to be healthy. In regard to doctrine, we use it to describe someone who is grounded, someone whose doctrinal foundation is firm and pure. We need to have a healthy belief, a sound faith. When we are doctrinally sound, we are safe people. Our fruit is pure, refreshing, the real deal, no artificial flavoring. When a younger woman comes to an older woman, she should be able to pick and eat from her basket without worry of food poisoning.

There is a dear woman in my community that I'm simply wild about. She is fearless. I've never met another woman like her. Her zeal for Christ is off the charts. Her name is probably on the lips of every prostitute and every lap and pole dancer in my town. She takes them cookies at Christmas and gifts of make-up and sundry needs. She brandishes the gospel like a knight with his sword. She goes around with the joy of the Lord on her lips and written all over her car in chalk. She is a wonder of God. She is sound in love. She is sound in perseverance. Doctrine? Not so much. I have never once doubted her worship of Christ, but I would not put my basket under her doctrinal tree for nourishment. My friend is healthy in many things, but her understanding of God and His ways is sometimes a little east of the King's highway, a little less than straight. It's crucial that we learn what God's word teaches. It's crucial that we learn to learn. Here are the ways in which Paul uses the word *sound*: sound doctrine, sound words of our Lord Jesus Christ, sound teaching, sound in the faith, sound speech, sound in love, sound in steadfastness. Soundness is important.

When God calls us to be healthy in faith, He is instructing us to cultivate a healthy belief system, as well as healthy obedience. Healthy faith believes rightly *and* obeys the truth. This demands we be veracious Bible readers, believers, and doers. In other words, be a Christian. Ear-tickling teachers who never use the words *sin, repent, suffering, or humility* should repulse us. What suits our passions should not be the criteria we use to choose a church home. Not all Bible teachers teach the Bible and not all Christians endure sound teaching. I know some Christians that approach the Bible the way they approach their medical quirks. It's like using the internet to diagnose an illness. Here's my unseemly example:

I struggle with a weird disease that mainly torments my digestive system. A multitude of things set off episodes: stress, lack of sleep, environmental factors like smells, stress, not eating or eating the wrong foods at the wrong time, stress, heat, cold hardware stores, ants, gnats, grumpy people, and did I mention stress? I'm being a little cheeky. It seems as though my body is allergic to everything whenever it wants. I had one of these "gastronomical" episodes on a 19-hour road trip to Oklahoma where, ironically, I was traveling to de-stress. A flare caused loss of sleep, which led to not eating, which caused another flare, and so it goes. I chose my best option. Don't judge. Pretzels and pink liquid gels. The pink stuff helped, although I spent several hours in the car trying to get this particular brand's annoying jingle out of my head. When I arrived at my brother's home, I felt significantly better.

Unseemliness alert: I awoke to a bowel movement that, I jest not, was black. Super black. Coal black. Freaky black. I did what I knew not to do: Website. Type "black stool." Enter. Every article I read screamed, "You are bleeding internally! Go to the ER!" At least, that's the way I interpreted it. Stress. I reached for my bottle of Children's Benadryl (grape), swigged and swallowed. And then, hidden at the end of an article, I read these words: "taking iron pills, activated charcoal, or medicines that contain bismuth [like in the pink stuff] can cause black stools." Inhale followed by a long exhale. Imagine handling the Bible like WebWhatAilsYou.com. If I were to put the symptoms of my particular disease into the "search" on a medical webpage, I would probably get thirty different diagnoses. Okay, so I did it. At this very moment, I could be suffering from flu, cholera, salmonella, IBS, food poisoning, food allergy, just poisoning, appendicitis, colon cancer, gastritis, altitude sickness, parasites, and my favorite – the plague. Not exactly a sound diagnosis. Or a sound way of finding what ails you.

We shouldn't treat the Bible as a search engine for what ails us. I'm not saying it's always bad to find a Scripture for what ails you. In fact, I recommend it. I'm a firm believer in preaching to yourself and listening to the word of God. Verses often come to mind when I need them. They are good medicine to my soul, good weapons against my own flesh, the world, and the adversary. What *am* I saying? It's not healthy to pick and choose willy-nilly through the word of God like we are buying socks. It might encourage you to be a disobedient oaf and to never take a bath. "Let the one who does wrong, still do wrong; and the one who is filthy, still be filthy" (Rev. 22:1). Taken out of context, a guy could start the Church of the Unrepentant and Unbaptized. To be sound in faith and doctrine is to know and trust the whole counsel of God's word. It's to know and trust Christ Himself for the remedy to all of our infirmities, spiritual and physical. His diagnosis is true. His cure is perfectly sufficient. The Bible was not meant to be just a way to bandage a scratch, diagnose ourselves, or even to improve ourselves. In it we find Christ is all we need for life and godliness. Everything we need, in Christ we possess.[45] Many of us tend toward spiritual anorexia. We seldom eat from the word, and when we do, it's because we are desperate. "Man shall not live on bread alone, but on *every* word that proceeds out of the mouth of God" (Matt. 4:4). Every word, not just the ones that sound nice to us. We need the whole loaf, the whole counsel of God's word, with a rich, consistent diet.

Sound In Love

We are also encouraged to be sound in love. The Bible gives us vivid expressions of Christian love:

---

[45] Thanks Cindy.

> *You shall love the Lord your God with all your heart, and with all your soul, and with all your mind. Matthew 22:37*
>
> *You shall love your neighbor as yourself. Matthew 22:39*
>
> *Love your enemies and pray for those who persecute you. Matthew 5:44*
>
> *A new commandment I give to you, that you love one another; even as I have loved you, that you also love one another. By this all men will know that you are My disciples, if you have love for one another. John 13:34-35*
>
> *If anyone loves Me, he will keep My word, and My Father will love him, and We will come to him and make Our abode with him. John 14:23*
>
> *If you keep my commandments, you will abide in My love, just as I have kept My Father's commandments and abide in His love. John 15:10*
>
> *Love does no wrong to a neighbor; therefore love is the fulfillment of the law. Romans 13:10*
>
> *Love is patient, love is kind and is not jealous; love does not brag and is not arrogant, does not act unbecomingly; it does not seek its own, is not provoked, does not take into account a wrong suffered, does not rejoice in unrighteousness, but rejoices with the truth; bears all things, believes all things, hopes all things, endures all things. Love never fails. 1 Corinthians 13:4-8a*

Sound love sets God as supreme treasure and delight. We love with *all* our heart, *all* our soul, *all* our mind, *all* our strength. We are commanded to do this. This kind of love is not our default setting. Love must be intentional. The command assumes we know God, that we seek Him, that we meditate in the Scriptures to know and understand His ways. We behold Him and ruminate on who He is, asking and asking and asking Him to teach us to love Him.

Sound love is obedient love, love that wants to please Christ. It is authentic and finds its source in Christ alone. It's a fruit of the Spirit, worked into us by Him. We love others, not considering whether they desire it or return it. Rather, we love because He first loved us. It is both our duty and our privilege. Sound love is wholehearted and unselfish. Older women are to exemplify it and teach it. Why? It's good.

Sound In Steadfastness

Did you know there is such a thing as *unsound* steadfastness? Watch the woman who grits her teeth and endures without letting trials touch her heart. She has little compassion because "by gosh, if I have to endure it, so do you." She's the one saying, "just deal with it. Suck it up" or the gauche expression (drives me bananas when I hear it), "just put on your big girl panties." This is the woman that suffers in bitterness and silence. Sound steadfastness is altogether different. More truly, it is to suffer well, to remain under trials and suffering until they produce the result for which God designed them. To be sound in steadfastness is to display the quality of character that doesn't surrender to circumstance, but does surrender to Jesus in the circumstance. Sound steadfastness doesn't grow weary in doing good (Ro. 2:7); instead, it rejoices in suffering and produces character and hope (Ro. 5:3-5). It results in God's sufficient and gracious comfort (2 Cor. 1:6). We participate in a steadfastness that doesn't even belong to us – it belongs to Christ (2 Th. 3:5). When we are sound in steadfastness (or perseverance), we become mature; we are complete, lacking nothing (James 1:2-4). Healthy steadfastness is endurance while looking up. It doesn't whine, moan, or grumble. It's based upon the sound doctrine of God's sovereignty, that He governs all things and gives what He deems necessary to mold us into the image of His Son, empowering us to remain upright under it. Teach what is sound, older women, and encourage others to be healthy in their doctrine, faith, love, and perseverance.

Someone Is Watching

Good lessons learned under Jesus' tutelage is a prerequisite for training others, that is, unless the goal is to cause stumbling. We have it within us to train young women to be foolish without even trying. This instruction to teach what is good assumes that older women *know* what is good. Then it assumes they will teach what is good. It doesn't assume the gift of teaching, but it does assume older women will teach. What we have to pass along can be either good or bad. This command doesn't excuse us if we are busy. It doesn't excuse us if we didn't sign up for the mentoring program. It doesn't excuse us if we are introverts. It doesn't excuse us if we are forty-five, sixty, or ninety-nine. This exhortation does not excuse us if we "paid our dues" in the church nursery or on the youth trip way-back-when. Paul only assumes we are older than some of the women in our church, that we are Christians, and that we will teach.

Creepy or not, someone is watching. I promise. We are teaching whether we know it or not. And women will decide, based upon our behavior, whether God and His word can really be trusted or whether it can really bring satisfaction and blessing. Good things are those things that approve or commend the word of God as a life source. The Bible looks good (and is good). God is good and our behavior should show that He is.

Consider this, reader. If a young single woman were to watch you with your spouse, do you think she might want to be married? What is she seeing? Are you a stay-at-home mom? Would a young, single woman want a job or kids like yours someday? Think with me. Would a young woman want the kind of relationship you have with the Lord Jesus? Would she want to know how you've struggled with sin and died to it? Would she want to learn from you how to pray? Would she think your kindness or your hospitality was worthy of imitation? Would she want you to help her steward her resources? Does she believe she could share her heart with you? Might she think, "It's a mystery to me how she seems to know where to find things in her Bible." In your suffering and sickness, in the headaches and the rough stuff, would she marvel that you are steadfast in your faith? Are you teaching a life of good things by your deeds – things that prove the goodness of God to you in your own life?

Or might she think, "Why would I want *that?*" Tough marriage? Is your life teaching that God is good in the midst of it, that He sustains you and sanctifies you and gives you His peace and joy? Or does it teach marriage is just too hard and too ugly. Ornery children? Is your life teaching that God is a good, patient, consistent, and compassionate parent? Or does it teach that children are too much responsibility, that they steal your life and joy? Are there insane family situations you are trying to traverse? Is your life teaching that Jesus brings balance even in the tsunami,[46] that He is more than sufficient and lavishes peace and grace in the center of the storm? Or does your response teach dark times call for dark emotions – anger, depression, complaining, backbiting, revenge?

We aren't to just go about our lives quietly hoping that a few good things seep through to on-lookers. What others witness is a form of teaching, so we are commanded to teach good things with our mouths, hands, feet, and attitudes. This means resolve and a humble dependence upon the Lord, and knowing what is good.

Most of the women I encounter are looking for meaning or significance. Older Christian woman – that's our fault, mine and yours. We women in the faith have not always imaged Christian womanhood as beautiful and satisfying to our sisters. Women are drawn to the workplace (granted, some are forced into it) and to men and to internet gurus and to books and to oodles of other things for meaning because they don't understand or believe that their God-designed role is enough to satisfy. How could being a helper to my husband be enough to give God glory? Many of us started having children and pushed an invisible HOLD button saying to ourselves,

---

[46] Why can't we just drop the "t"?

"When I get these rascals raised, then I'll work on being somebody," as if we weren't already somebody – someone smack in the middle of God's will, doing incredibly difficult stuff for an incredibly gracious God who is nodding with pleasure that we love our children and husbands more than we love ourselves. Be a teacher of good things so that the word of God will not be dishonored.

Are you an older woman? Teach, girl, and do it with gusto. I'm preaching at this moment to myself. I'm not sure that in the last few years any young woman would want me as an example. I do not say this lightly. I think I've taught some good things. But as I type this, I'm thinking about what I haven't taught well. I'm pretty serious. I don't teach the joy of the Lord well. I struggle with chronic illness that will, from the look of things, never be taken from me until I meet Jesus face-to-face. I'm striving to teach perseverance, but I'm still growing up in it. Paul doesn't give me or you an *out*. He doesn't say, "Older women, when you get your act together, teach." This is a *here a little, there a little,* precept upon precept, life work. We can't assume we have nothing to teach (or to learn). God is good and good to us. Teach that.

Finally, if you are older than fifty-five, like me you are on the downhill (so I'm told). You have more years behind than before. I rather think of it as headed uphill and closer to the zenith than others. There's no coasting on the uphill. In fact, the closer to the top, the slower the climb and the thinner the air. This is not the time to binge on "somedays." We don't have the promise of tomorrow, let alone someday. This is the time to push into the lives of younger women, to say I've been there, done that, don't even need the t-shirt because God's grace and fruit are enough to give me a bit of kingdom street cred. It's time to say, "Let me help you" and to let more mature women teach us. If you are near the top of the mountain, but surmise you are still too immature, it's not too late. Be taught. Open your Bible, repent, and believe. Grow up. "Like newborn babies, long for the pure milk of the word, so that by it you may grow in respect to salvation" (1 Pet. 2:2). "But grow in the grace and knowledge of our Lord and Savior Jesus Christ" (2 Pet. 3:18a). Are you an older woman who has never married? We need you. Are you a widow? We need you. We need you to do your kingdom duty. We need to see you worship. We need to hear you pray. We need God's wisdom and kindness to pass over your lips. We need your encouragement. We need you to be brave and step into the lives of women around you. I hope if you are a younger woman, you can say, "Amen."

I'm setting my face toward Christ, resolved to keep climbing for His sake and to make sure that the rope is firm and taut for my grand-girls, my daughter, and any women coming behind me. My pen may be my greatest tool for that, but I still hope to be more visible. When women look into my "window," I hope they see a woman intent on pleasing Christ, a woman bent on glorifying God in my home, in my marriage, as a parent and grandparent, in my friendships, in my behavior, in my attitudes, in my words, and in my work. I hope they see me pressing into all I do with the full assurance that this role, this call of Christian womanhood, is a gift. It is God's pleasure. It is lovely. It is enough. May God teach us to keep the curtains open and to teach good things to our sisters and daughters in Christ so that the word of God will be magnified as supremely true.

Chapter 8

Restored to Our Senses

Older women likewise are to be reverent in their behavior, not malicious gossips nor enslaved to much wine, teaching what is good, ***so that they may encourage* [train] *the young women...***

Titus 2:3-4a

Train And Be Trained

I never liked the word "train" unless it was in relation to locomotives or the pop rock group. Training requires self-discipline. It usually means arduous work. It might require sweat. I don't like sweat.[47] When I see women considering the military and "basic training" comes up, I internally caterwaul. "What are you thinking, woman? You don't have to do that to your mind and body!" Middle child of a career military man, I can still hear the rhythmic stomping of airmen running in time on the bases where we lived, singing some manly-men songs (sometimes crude), echoing their leader. I'm grateful for soldiers, and I admire fit people, but I've never admired them enough to get fit. That's just me.

The training Paul mentions here is not an option. Christian women are enlisted as either a trainer or a trainee with the goal to someday train. This training is wholly other than the aforementioned sweat fest. The word

[47] My husband's grandmother always said that "men sweat, children perspire and women dew." I don't even like to "dew."

translated *train* (or *encourage* in the NASB) in the Bible is the verb form of *sensible* which we will look at more closely later. Though some Bible versions, including the one I'm using, translate this word as *encourage,* it has a much richer meaning. It contains earnestness. It means to disciple or to hold someone to their duty. The elder women are literally instructed to restore younger women to their senses, to help them cultivate sound judgment and prudence. This is why some versions translate this verse by saying something like the *King James Version,* "That they may teach the young women to be sober."

God is calling women to sane living, "to be restored to our senses, to have a sane mind." I can't count the times I've heard women say, "My husband is driving me crazy." "My children are driving me insane." "My world is nuts." We get overwhelmed. Sometimes sanity seems frightfully frail. Some women who stay home struggle with cabin fever. They feel lonely, isolated, and sub-par even if they are surrounded by family and friends. Their FaceBook page is deceptively filled with shiny, happy faces. Some women outside the home struggle with guilt. We all struggle with feeling frazzled and fatigued. We are pulled between various loyalties: parents, husband, children, friends, jobs, sports leagues, and so on. We've been convinced we just need self-care and self-actualization, fulfillment and success.

I recognize these struggles are not imagined, but we need to learn what to pick up and what to let alone. Many of these pressures can be relieved through godly training. Training is the process of bringing God's word to bear on every aspect of life. We women have to learn to choose the good part (Luke 10:42). We want to learn to ask, "What *is* important? What has Jesus called me to focus on? What does God value?" This is what I think it means to have our senses restored to us. We evaluate our lives, not by what others think or what we've always been taught or by new trends or by the latest Christian podcast. We evaluate and prioritize within God's economy. In other words, "How am I, a Christian, to live? What does the Bible say? What does God esteem?" God esteems the character of His Son alive and working in His children, working in His daughters, flowing out into our families, church family, communities, and ultimately into the world.

"Let our sons in their youth be as grown-up plants, and our daughters as corner pillars fashioned as for a palace" (Ps. 144:12). Women are trained to be caryatids. Talk about strength and beauty! Take a field trip on the internet and look at caryatids. They are magnificent marble pillars carved into stately female sculptures holding the ceiling of a palace on their heads. Strong. Unflappable. Essential. Indispensable support at home and in the house of God.

Restored To Our Senses

Recently I witnessed the complete opposite of a trained, sane woman. I was leaving a little eatery. It was early morning and, except for the crazy scene in the parking lot, quiet. In the parking lot, right next to my car, was a 20-something woman punching the driver door on her car. I thought she must have locked her keys in the car and was taking it out on the door. I watched her (from afar) put on her jacket, open the door and enter her car. She wasn't locked out. "Oh good," I thought. I took a few steps closer. She exited her car, screamed obscenities into her phone, threw the phone into the seat, slammed the door, ripped off her jacket again, screamed vulgarities and obscenities, and yes, beat her SUV senseless. She put her jacket back on. Press repeat. This went on for fifteen minutes. I wanted to help her, but found it hard to interrupt. I mean, she had a routine. I thought if I engaged her, she might consider it an act of war. I got into my car. She looked at me and went back to her routine. I bowed my head and prayed for her. I was sad for her. She was lost in so many ways. She got in her car and drove off. Fast. She was completely out of her mind, sharing her insanity with some poor soul on the phone, the diners, me, and all of Oklahoma. She was an unhinged palooka, lost as a goose in a rainstorm. She needed restoration first, and then her senses righted, trained in godliness. I'm still praying for you, young lady, wherever you are.

This brings to my mind Mary Magdalene. We don't know much about her, but at the beginning of Luke 8 we read: "Soon afterwards, He *began* going around from one city and village to another, proclaiming and preaching the kingdom of God. The twelve were with Him, and *also* some women who had been healed of evil spirits and sicknesses: Mary who was called Magdalene, from whom seven demons had gone out…" At some point in time, she was the bed and breakfast for seven evil spirits. Dr. Abraham Kuyper did a character assessment of her. He might have been talking about me, minus the "seven demons" thing:

> *Mary Magdalene is Peter's feminine counterpart in the circle which followed Jesus. Both were characterized by much zeal and fervor, and in both that fervor sometimes leaped over its appropriate boundaries; it became impetuosity and had to be punished… Magdala, Mary's natal town, was situated about three miles from Capernaum. Hence, it is not surprising that she soon heard about Jesus and came into direct contact with Him. That is especially true because she was a conspicuous figure in Magdala. She was a comparatively rich woman, but she had been most cruelly subjected to the influence of devils. Seven devils had made her personality their seat. There are some who infer from this fact that she was an adulterous woman. That is by no means a necessary implication. She had nothing in common with the repentant sinner who washed Jesus' feet. But we may safely infer from the fact that she was possessed of devils that she was by nature very passionate and impetuous. Such persons are most susceptible to the influence of devils, and all such spiritual qualms arise from a sinful condition of the human heart. But Mary had finally been purged of these influences. She had gone to Jesus. Jesus understood her, because He observed that faith was mingled with her passionate petitions. Then He became her Saviour and cast seven devils out of her. After that moment, Mary's passionate fervor, just*

> *as did Peter's, directed itself to but a single end. She dedicated her life to Jesus as a sacrifice of thanksgiving.*[48]

Ever felt like your fervor just leapt over the appropriate boundary? I can raise my hand. That was me. Granted, Kuyper used some liberty by filling in the blanks of her story, but he could be right. Later, we find Mary Maggie in three of the gospels announcing the empty tomb. Mark tells us that others refused to believe her. We do know from this account that "after He [Jesus] had risen early on the first day of the week, He first appeared to Mary Magdalene, from whom He had cast out seven demons" (Mark 16:9-11). You know what strikes me? Everyone knew about the seven demons. After the "come to Jesus" moment, there must have been an obvious "come to her senses" transformation.

In Mark 5 there is another encounter that might give us an idea of what Mary Magdalene is all about.

> *They came to the other side of the sea, into the country of the Gerasenes. When He got out of the boat, immediately a man from the tombs with an unclean spirit met Him, and he had his dwelling among the tombs. And no one was able to bind him anymore, even with a chain; because he had often been bound with shackles and chains, and the chains had been torn apart by him and the shackles broken in pieces, and no one was strong enough to subdue him. Constantly, night and day, he was screaming among the tombs and in the mountains, and gashing himself with stones. Seeing Jesus from a distance, he ran up and bowed down before Him; and shouting with a loud voice, he said, "What business do we have with each other, Jesus, Son of the Most High God? I implore you by God, do not torment me!" For He had been saying to him, "Come out of the man, you unclean spirit!" And He was asking him, "What*

[48] Abraham Kuyper, *Women of the New Testament* (Michigan: Zondervan, 1963), 32-33.

> *is your name?" And he said to Him, "My name is Legion; for we are many."*

After Jesus cast the demons into a herd of swine, the people heard and returned. This is what followed:

> *They came to Jesus and observed* ***the man who had been demon-possessed sitting down, clothed and in his right mind,*** *the very man who had had the "legion"...*

We don't get to know this man's name. Later we find that he wanted to accompany Jesus, but Jesus told him no. Mary Maggie was apparently free to follow. There she was, released from bondage, no more demons, seven evictions. Can you imagine her weeping, straightening her hair and her dress, sitting down and resting with Jesus, finally in her right mind, finally having come to her senses? From that point on she is a womanly force to be reckoned with. All of the disciples except John ran from the scene when Christ was crucified. Not Mary Magdalene. She stayed. She watched. She served. Kuyper, at the end of his sketch, speaks of her this way:

> *Not every woman of Jesus' circle was as passionate as that. Mary of Nazareth was different, Salome was very different from that, and so was Martha, Lazarus' sister. But a fervent nature, and the zeal of feminine ardor had to be represented in that group of women. It was represented in those good things she did, but it was also represented in her undue impetuosity. It was represented in her, in order that our Saviour could be refreshed by such ardor and in order that He could temper an exaggeration of it. The situation in Jesus' Church is no different from what it was in His little circle. The Church may not snub the Magdalenes.*[49]

[49] Ibid.

When Jesus sent her out on that resurrection day, He showed the world that Mary was more than her demons. She was more than her exorcism. She was a daughter of Christ the King heralding life eternal.

Behold Jesus

Mary Magdalene and the Gerasene man point us to where training starts. It always begins with beholding Jesus. Salvation restores our senses. Our Father is the source of our sanity, of our restoration. As His children, we begin there as well. We ask, "What does Father say about this?" Get a picture in your head of Sunday morning at your local church. Now focus in on the women. Think about their personalities. Their ages, their social station and interests, their careers, hobbies, gifts, and skills. See their faces and smiles and frowns and fear and sadness and joy and excitement. Are they mature? Are they newly restored Mary Maggies? Now put yourself in the picture with them. Are you old or young? What does Titus 2 say to you? Train or be trained? You are standing in a field of women who need you either way, and you need them.

Why are we to train them in all things Jesus? So that the word of God may not be dishonored (or reviled, Titus 2:5). As true as it is that we are not to slander others in our speech, we are not to slander God's word by a life that ignores His truth and will. What we say and do as women in our homes, in our families, in our neighborhoods, and in our churches genuinely matters. God says we are to teach what is good and train young women how to be Christian women so that their lives (behavior, speech, emotions, thoughts, deeds), won't disparage the reputation of the Christ they mirror to others. Instead, by every aspect of our lives, we prove the truth of God's word and Christ's character in us.

Like the bondslaves mentioned in 2:9, Titus 2:10 calls us to "adorn the doctrine of God our Savior in every respect." Think about what it means to *adorn* something. Women are particularly suited for this service. We like to beautify things. We are made to make things "gooder."[50] To adorn is to put something beautiful or attractive on display. The doctrine of God is beautiful. We should long for others to view the gospel of God, to view redemption, justification, sanctification, glorification as beautiful and worthy of our gratitude. It is the very beauty of Christ our Lord and Savior. To adorn His doctrine is to adorn Him, to put Him on display for the world to see His enormous value and beauty. This command to train other women is a call to teach women to direct everything in their lives to praise the Lord and bring Him glory, showing Him as He is: beautiful.

Women in the church, from the Mary Magdalenes to the Annas, need you. Our heavenly Father is interested in His character flowing from the personalities we've each been given, in the places we've been planted, with the gifts we've been granted, by the grace, mercy and love He has lavished on us, by His Spirit who dwells within us. He has chosen to use the woman next to you in the pew, and He has chosen you to behold Him, to believe Him, and to encourage other women to do the same. It's a barefoot moment. We look away from ourselves, chins lifted to the face of Christ, and *then* we stoop to wash the feet of the women around us. We repent of our fear, insecurity and apathy so that, in humility, we can graciously allow other women to do the same for us. Our training is not first done in the confines of Bible studies and small groups. The prerequisite of training is relationship: a relationship with Christ, and *then* friendships and communion with others.

Lots of women are quirky, like me. I've met all sorts: self-controlled, unfiltered, unapproachable, gregarious, know-it-alls, humble, biblically illiterate, scholarly, gentle, abrupt, zealous, quiet. God hasn't called us to fix them or prejudge them. We aren't to despise them if they don't see things in the same way. We love them, so we train them.

> *Therefore if there is any encouragement in Christ, if there is any consolation of love, if there is any fellowship of the Spirit, if any affection and compassion, make my joy complete by*

---

[50] This is my son's favorite way of describing what it means to glorify something. I like it.

> *being of the same mind, maintaining the same love, united in spirit, intent on one purpose. Do nothing from selfishness or empty conceit, but with humility of mind regard one another as more important than yourselves; do not merely look out for your own personal interests, but also for the interests of others. Have this attitude in yourselves which was also in Christ Jesus.*
> *Philippians 2:1-5*

Even though other women may not be like you, they are vital to you. Let's not snub the Mary Maggie's of the church. Let's train them. Let's lead them to the source of sober, sane, restored senses. Jesus will have them sitting up, dressed, and in their right minds in no time.

Chapter 9

Husband-Lover

> *Older women likewise are to be reverent in their behavior, not malicious gossips nor enslaved to much wine, teaching what is good, so that they may encourage the young women to* ***love their husbands...***
>
> *Titus 2:3-4a*

I had just had a complete makeover, and I was looking my finest. I was twenty-one and a worldling on my way to Hell, doing my best to get there with a smile. My brother wanted me to meet his friend at the fast-food restaurant that he managed. There was my husband-to-be, though I didn't know it, wearing a silly hat, cleaning out the shake machine. I've loved him ever since.

Neither of us had a brain in our heads back then. And neither of us was a Christian. After we were married, Christ introduced Himself. The new parameters helped. Our marriage wasn't great, but as Christians, we understood it was permanent. Several times in our marriage we reached a place where we said, "It's a covenant. Divorce is not an option. Now what?" We took God's side on our marriage. It held us. Looking back, I think vows should include something like this: "I, Jon, a sinner, take you, Denise, a sinner, to be my lawful wedded wife forever" and "I, Denise, a sinner, take you, Jon, a sinner, to be my lawful wedded husband forever." We really should know what we are getting into.

I joke that every five to seven years, I wake up next to a new man. Jon and I are not even close to the people we were when we got married. We don't think the same. We don't believe the same. We don't even kiss the same.[51] And thankfully, we don't love the same. By the grace of God, our marriage has been rocked, shaken, broken, mended, and molded into a gift neither of us would give up… ever. We discovered who keeps our marriage, and it's not us. I've discovered that the worst sinner in the marriage is me and he has discovered that the worst sinner in the marriage is him. We've discovered that the best one in the marriage is Christ. So, we are committed to doing things His way. We love each other by esteeming one another as better than ourselves (most of the time), giving rather than taking, and by following the guidelines God has given, staying in our respective lanes. We are forty years in.

Before I get sucked down the marriage talk hole, let me begin here: if you are single or if you are widowed, this command to "love your husband" is not as irrelevant to you as you might think. Write these on your mirror: John 15:1-14, John 21:15-17, 1 John 4:7-21 and Isaiah 54:5. You have a husband. If God gives you an earthly one, rejoice and be glad, but don't think you've been short-changed right now. There is no better husband and head than Jesus Christ Himself.

Love Your Husbands

Titus 2 commands older women to teach the younger women to love their husbands. Why do Christian women need to be discipled to do something that seems to come with the whole female package? Men are often commanded in Scripture to love their wives, but wives are seldom told to love their husbands. Don't most women love their husbands and children? Why do we need to be "restored to our senses" in this area?

I know some women would say, "I would take a grenade for my children" and some of them might even take a bullet for their husbands, if they had

[51] False teeth. Nuf said.

to. Some husbands can be stinkers. Some wives too. The instruction here is to teach younger women to (literally) "be into their husbands." We are to be fond of them, be affectionate to them. We may *love* them, but God wants us to love them His way and to love them well.

As a child, I can say with veracity that I never felt "liked" or particularly "loved." Well into my teens, I believed that there was something desperately wrong with me, so wrong that naturally people couldn't love me. Many years later, I had an encounter with God through His word in 2 Samuel 22. This verse seemed mysteriously highlighted: "He [God] brought me out into a broad place; He rescued me, because He delighted in me" (v. 20). This was a total mystery to me. My first thought was "Yeah, God has to love me. He's God." But then I started digging into that verse. I looked up the word *delighted* and was almost giddy. This is how it's related in my journal: *God rescued me, not because His love demanded Him to, but because He simply likes me. Father is fond of me.*

He is fond of you. It makes a world of difference in a girl when she finds out her heavenly Father likes her. This sort of affection is catchy. To this day, I am incredibly fond of my husband and children. I would want to be their friends if I couldn't be related to them. I would still catch a grenade for them. Certainly, I love them to the moon and back. But with all of that, when we get together, I feel like I finally get to sit at the cool table with friends.

Love Is Respect

Christian women are to be Christ-lovers and husband-lovers. What about husbands? They are commanded to love their wives just as Christ loved the church, giving themselves up for their brides. Ephesians 5 says this of husbands three times in nine verses. God wants him to get it. But here is what He says to us, young and old wives, in the last of those same nine verses: "and let the wife see that she respects her husband" (Eph. 5:33).

The fond affection that we have for our husbands is highlighted in our respect for them. We women can naturally love a man even though we may not honor or respect him very much. This is called a problem. Husbands need respect like a car needs fuel. We need love in the same way, but listen, sister, we can't just give our husband what *we* need. Loving him well means respecting him.

Respect is a difficult thing to define. It looks different in various relationships. It means to esteem a husband with a wholesome, godly reverence because of his office, his position as head over his wife. We do not honor husbands the way a slave serves a master. Instead, a wife honors her husband like a crown honors a king. Kings don't always deserve respect, but the crown doesn't care.

I must come clean. It's taken many years of marriage for me to get in the Biblical respect groove. Male role models were lacking in my family. But my mother was one of the most gracious women I've ever known. She respected my father for years when there appeared to be nothing to respect. I labeled her a victim very early on and swore to never let a man walk over me like my father did her. Now I am so very grateful for her hard-won example of respect in action and the gracious sweep of her white robe of righteousness that I know was being woven. I was wrong. She wasn't weak.

I have a husband who is worthy of respect. He makes it easy for me, but it hasn't always been that way. I think a man respected by his wife will become more respectable. The same is true for a woman loved rightly. They become lovely. Maybe your husband is a hard man to respect. It doesn't matter. Remember, the crown sits on the head whether it's deserved or not. If we have to have a reason, we start by respecting our husband's position. Whether we like it or not, God seems to esteem hierarchy. He approves of order. When I voluntarily come under the headship of my husband, I shine the crown on his head. This is respect. What does it look like "in real life?"

We respect our husband's leadership. Jon and I have agreed that our relationship in regard to large decisions is not equal, but it's not unjust. We look at it as a 51% to 49% partnership. Someone has to have the final say. Two heads on a body is a monster. God gives that *say* to our husbands. My husband frequently asks my advice. He doesn't always take it, but I trust Christ in him. That's taken time, but he has proven to lead me well. Yes, he has made mistakes. In those times, I learned to trust Christ to lead us out of them. He has made a few sinful choices. In those times, I learned to duck and not get in the way of God's discipline when it was warranted. I can honestly say I never chafe anymore under his leadership. In fact, I find myself delighting in it as we get older and resting in the security it brings. His leadership is for my good.

We respect our husband's provision for us. I'm not so cut off from the world that I don't realize many women in our churches are in the workforce, either by choice, need, or because their husbands expect it. We will get to the subject of being "workers at home" later, but what I want to emphasize now is the responsibility of a woman to respect what her husband provides for her. Is the paycheck he brings home stewarded well by you? Do you use well the resources that he has provided for you? What about your home? Do you show him your gratitude by keeping it in working order and keeping it clean, useful, and inviting? In other words, be content and grateful for the provision God has made for you through him.

We respect our husband's reputation. We like a good joke around our house, but humor or snark tears down a man, especially in front of his peers. It is a neon sign of disrespect. Jon used to jokingly say, "I'm the head, but Denise is the neck. She turns me wherever she wants." I hated that joke. And I told him so. It wasn't – and still isn't – true. I work hard at honoring him and try to afford him the same courtesy. We need to esteem our husbands before others, and what we say needs to be the truth. My husband is a deacon in our local church. The best one, by the way. As such, part of respecting his reputation is to emulate what the Bible requires of deacons' wives: dignity, not malicious gossips, temperate, and faithful in all things (1 Tim. 3:11) and since deacons are to be good managers of their children and their own households, I respect him by helping him manage our household (and me) well. Occasionally, my role might be as simple as reminding him to fix his face. He forgets to smile sometimes. We want their crowns to shine, ladies, especially in the gates.

We respect our husband's virility. He's a man. He's masculine. And he likes it. So should we. My son was researching the art of hospitality. He ran across one of Emily Post's books. In it she was discussing the carrying of "bundles" and my son took her advice to heart. The main point was that a woman should not carry more than one bundle; a man should help her if she has more than one. Now the definition of bundle was important. For instance, it would be disrespectful for me to ask my husband to carry my fuzzy pink stuffed bunny for me in public.[52] For a bit of snarky comic relief:

> *Nearly all books on etiquette insist that a "gentleman must offer to carry a lady's bundles." Bundles do not suggest a lady in the first place, and as for gentlemen and bundles! – they don't go together at all. Very neat packages that could never without injury to their pride be designated as "bundles" are different. Such, for instance, might be a square, smoothly wrapped box of cigars, candy, or books. Also, a gentleman might carry flowers, or a basket of fruit, or, in fact, any package that looks tempting. He might even stagger under bags and suitcases, or a small trunk – but carry a "bundle"? Not twice! And yet, many an unknowing woman, sometimes a very young and pretty one, too, has asked a relative, a neighbor, or an admirer, to carry something suggestive of a pillow, done up in crinkled paper and odd lengths of joined string. Then she wonders afterwards in unenlightened surprise why her cousin, or her neighbor, or her admirer, who is one of the smartest men in town, never comes to see her anymore!*[53]

What she's saying is froufrou items can cause a man to look effeminate. Think about that the next time you ask your husband to carry your box of Tampons for you. We now have men in our family that are very aware of

[52] I don't have a pink fuzzy stuffed bunny, but if I did, I would never ask Jon to surrender his "man-card" to carry it for me.

[53] Emily Post, *Etiquette* (New York: Funk & Wagnalls, 1922).

how many "bundles" their wives are sporting, what kind they are, and they carry the extras (as long as they are not characteristically female bundles). Their man-credentials are strengthened when they use physical strength in the presence of their brides. At the risk of going too far, I don't generally get my husband greeting cards. He doesn't know what to do with them. I've started creating *man-cards,* useful and reusable. I've given him special occasion messages on everything from sand paper to car deodorizers to boot jacks. Respect your husband's manliness in whatever way best esteems him.

We respect our husband's need for friendship. I have a pet peeve. I don't like to have conversations from room to room. I have to see the face, and screaming at one another from room to room is an extreme irritation for me. Jon likes to talk while he walks, even in the house. He has gotten better, but he still does it. We both need to know that we've been heard. Often respect means I follow him from room to room, if need be, and when he does finally land somewhere, to stop what I'm doing and listen to what he has to say, even if I don't want to listen to the virtues of hops and yeast in beer. Try to find common likes. We've had to work hard on that one. We have a motorcycle and take rides together. We love good bourbon and good music. We're finding our way. I encourage you, young women, to not wait so long.

He also needs time with other men. Our church has a Men's Theology Forum monthly. Our men go and listen to a speaker, discuss theological topics, and share bourbon, beer, and burns (cigars, pipes, cigarettes). It's been a great way to get to know men in the church and men in the community. My husband has talents that draw men to him. He rides motorcycles with men he works with. He brews beer in our basement and regularly has men over to "sit around the fire, spit and tell war stories." Men need other men as much as women need other women. Encourage your husband to build godly friendships.

> *An excellent wife is the crown of her husband, but she who shames him is like rottenness in his bones. Proverbs 12:4*

> *The heart of her husband trusts in her, and he will have no lack of gain. Proverbs 31:11*

> *Her husband is known in the gates, when he sits among the elders of the land. Proverbs 31:23*

We respect our husbands through physical affection. In our culture, sex is more than a hot topic; it's available for watching and buying. *Be careful little eyes what you see* has never been more cautionary in our technological big-top of phones, tablets, live stream, and cable in a culture that went from "if it feels good, do it" to "I felt like it, did it, and you should too." Sex is just a side order anymore. I can have my steak with a side order of perversion at the local Sports Café with twenty T.V.'s broadcasting. We are bombarded with sexualized images and messages announcing adultery is natural, fornication is fun, flirting is innocent, provocative dress is fashionable, homosexuality is normal, and Christians are prudes. Sex is either a free for all or a spectator sport. It's a sin-sick world.

Not so for the Christian. Jeremiah called Judah out. She had begun to look like the world. "Were they ashamed because of the abomination they had done? They certainly were not ashamed, and they did not know how to blush; therefore they shall fall among those who fall; at the time of their punishment they shall be brought down, says the LORD" (Jer. 8:12). What in the world, young woman, makes you blush? Does anything make you rush to the fast forward button or the EXIT on the remote? Do your cheeks burn and redden at the exposure of things out of sync with the truth of your Bible? The Bride of Christ ought to sport a holy blush in the presence of blatant sex gone amuck.

Why? Because sex was designed for Christians. It's ours. It's one of the best gifts God gave to His children. Not only is it meant for a holy purpose, it is also for our joy. Handed to believers in marriage as a gracious means of producing godly offspring, sex for the Christian is duty and pleasure, protection and wonder. It's a "no-blush zone" for the faithful husband and wife.

When we see others participating in it, we should feel deeply uncomfortable. We should blush because the marriage bed is to be honored.

Proverbs 30:18-19 lists four things that are "too wonderful": an eagle in the sky, a serpent on a rock (Lord, help my unbelief!), a ship in the middle of the sea, and *the way of a man with a maid*. Sex is a godly wonder. Outside of marriage, our abstinence is faithfulness. Inside of marriage our indulgence is faithfulness. When performed in honor, it puts love and beauty on display for the eyes of God and His "two-become-one" man and wife as they outdo one another in selflessness.

Sex is fun. It is meant to be pleasurable, not embarrassing or abhorrent. Children of God ought to be as pro-sex as we are pro-marriage between a man and a woman and pro-life where babies are concerned. "Let your fountain be blessed, and rejoice in the wife of your youth" (Prov. 5:18). In Genesis 26:8, Abimelech looks out of his window and sees Isaac *sporting* with Rebekah. This *sporting* was enough to reveal to him that Rebekah was more than just Isaac's sister. Various translations render Isaac's *sport* as laughing, showing endearment, caressing, fondling, playing, and (my personal favorite) dallying. In the words of one self-described puritan, this was some "holy horsing around." God has not simply approved sex inside of marriage. He has ordained it, stamped it, and commanded it for our delight. Sex in the context of godly marriage protects Christians from the perils of worldly sexual temptations. It deepens communion and fosters friendship and love.

Lest you think I don't understand that this is a difficult thing for some women (and more rarely, men), let me be as tastefully transparent as I can manage. Sex was ruined for me early on. My virginity was forcibly taken from me and, because of shame and my twisted ideas of right and wrong, I acquiesced like a slave to immorality for many years. Suffice it to say, I came with a truckload of baggage all labeled "handle with care," "fragile," "toxic," and "stand back when opening." I was a mess. What changed? I did, progressively, with help from our Lord. At some point, I discovered that it wasn't right for my husband to pay for my sins and the sins of those that sinned against me. I got good counsel and Father healed me, not overnight, but over time. Now sex is not something that I'm forced to endure. It's a gift and a delight. I wish I could chat with you face to face if this is your struggle. But know that the Lord is enough and all things, including sexual trauma, are within His reach to mend.

God has set some firm rules for sexual love. If you are not married, you are to be a locked garden to every man until you marry. Period. There's no excuse for sex outside of the marriage bed; even randy widows must get married. If you are married, you are to be sexually responsive to your husband. The garden should be wide open. This doesn't mean you have to embrace anything that is a perversion to you, but you are to be available to him.

> *The husband must fulfill his duty to his wife, and likewise also the wife to her husband. The wife does not have authority over her own body, but the husband does; and likewise also the husband does not have authority over his own body, but the wife does. Stop depriving one another, except by agreement for a time, so that you may devote yourselves to prayer, and come together again so that Satan will not tempt you because of your lack of self-control. 1 Corinthians 7:3-5*

God is calling us to exclusive intimacy. No other man gets to see you provocatively dressed. No other man is privy to your flirtation. And no other man gets to unlock the safe. We also have no right to change the combination to the safe every day, locking our husband out of that intimacy. We don't wield sex as a punishment or weapon because of anger or resentment.

I've mixed, mangled, and multiplied metaphors, but you get the picture. And again, we should also keep the garden from any pollution. Don't bring media (magazines, movies and videos) of any kind into your bedroom to "get into the mood." And absolutely don't bring an actual human being in to join the two of you. Oh. My. Word. No Christian in their right mind should even consider dishonoring the marriage bed through adultery or threesomes. I can't believe it even needs to be said. "Marriage is to be held in honor among all, and the marriage bed is to be undefiled; for fornicators and adulterers God will judge" (Heb. 13:4).

Adultery and fornication happen in the mind as well. Young women (and even some older women) have the propensity to fantasize about something wholly other than the world they've been given. Women love romance, the real and the fake. Many Christian women believe that what's been dubbed as "mommy porn" is okay. Smutty novels and beyond smutty novels are not for us. Don't indulge. They only breed discontentment and selfish entitlement. Trust me on this one. The mind is a playground and needs to be policed by the word of God, not infiltrated by the likes of shirtless fictional so-called heroes. Let your husband be your hero.

Finally, as an aside for women in the fall and winter of life, like me, I urge you to develop intimacy that can satisfy you in the absence of sex. Eventually, your body and his begin to break down, and the time will come when the intimacy of sex will wane. Cuddle now so you will cuddle later. Hold hands and hug now, so you will hold hands and hug later. We don't have to stop the appetizers just because the main course is no longer on the menu.

Are you married, Christian? Respect your husband. Enjoy love. God gave it to you. And when you see the gift perverted around you, be God's blushing bride. Learn to be a husband-lover and, in Christ, love well.

Chapter 10

Child-Lover

> *Older women likewise are to be reverent in their behavior, not malicious gossips nor enslaved to much wine, teaching what is good, so that they may encourage the young women to love their husbands,* ***to love their children…***
>
> *Titus 2:3-4*

I'm chuckling right now. I just went through every commentary I have on this verse of Scripture (and there are many), and not one of them expounds upon the last part of verse 4. Maybe those scholars thought, "I don't need to expound on women loving their children. They just do." But not all do, ladies. "Can a woman forget her nursing child and have no compassion on the son of her womb? *Even these may forget, but I will not forget you*" (Is. 49:15).[54] Only God Himself is a sure thing. It's not a given for moms. Apart from Christ, we are selfish creatures. I think parenting is one of God's greatest tools for weeding out selfishness in a woman. During the Covid-19 scare, when many parents were forced home, schools shut down, and children were forced to be educated on-line, mothers were flooding social media and bemoaning their plight. It wasn't always the loss of income, although that was absolutely an issue. Most of the frustration came from

---

[54] Italics mine.

not knowing what to do with their own children for eighteen hours a day.[55] The echo of "I can't wait to get my kids back to school" was not about their concern for uninterrupted education. It was to keep them from pulling out their own hair. I believe the love Paul speaks of here is not only the natural love that mothers have for their children. It's a call to love our children well, to love richly, deeply, selflessly. To love with God's love.

To love children well means loving them as the gifts they are. "Behold, children are a gift of the LORD, the fruit of the womb is a reward. Like arrows in the hand of a warrior, so are the children of one's youth. How blessed is the man whose quiver is full of them; they will not be ashamed when they speak with their enemies in the gate" (Ps. 127:3-5). Have you ever received an unfit gift? You know, it was thoughtful, but it wasn't something you would buy for yourself? Or everyone knows you like llamas, so that's all you ever get: llama journals, llama coasters, llama wall art, llama pajamas. Ten years later, you are still getting llamas even though you stopped liking llamas in 2014. Unfit gifts don't feel like gifts. I have ten grandchildren, and I labor over Christmas gifts starting in October. I want to make sure the gift is fit for each one of them. Last year, one of the ten seemed completely disappointed with the gift he had received. I thought, "Guess I'll need to do some investigating before his birthday rolls around." I didn't know him as well as I thought I did. The gift didn't fit him.

God has never once given me (or you) an unfit gift. He knows us to our very core, intimately. He knows what we want and need, and He also knows what our children want and need. Our children are fit for us – gifts straight from the hand of God, arrows in a sovereignly planned quiver. They are gifts given to us, fit for us, and designed for us to know, love, and steward. We are to receive them as such. They should be welcomed as treasures, not as inconveniences.

[55] The "pandemic" was also a blessing to some. Many women realized they could live on one income and that their children needed them. Many parents chose to continue homeschooling. School closures were actually a God-given mercy for many.

Our family was struggling. My husband was let go from his job. He picked up several odd jobs on various shifts to keep us afloat. We were emotionally and financially stretched. Then I got pregnant for the third time. I had a friend that worked at a crisis pregnancy center. I took my home pregnancy test to the center, handed it to her, and said, "I'm in crisis. This can't be right." She gave me another test. It was right. I said, "I can't go home and tell Jon I'm pregnant with all this going on!" She laughed and said, "Just tell him children are a gift from the Lord. The fruit of the womb is a reward. Psalm 127:3." I think my reply was something like, "I don't deserve a reward." When I got home, I did what my friend advised. I told Jon, "Now honey, children are a gift from the Lord and the fruit of the womb is a reward." His response: "It's not a gift – it's bad birth control." We were new to the faith.

By the time my son was born, I was "pondering" like Mary, Jesus' mother. We didn't owe a dime after his birth. Jon began a job that launched a lifetime career. Turned out the timing was perfect. Right after he was born, as I held him, Jon and I dubbed him *Lucas Andrew*. I believe God whispered in my ear, "A double disciple. He'll be a pastor." There were a few years there where I doubted that I had heard God right. I kept that secret until after his ordination. My gift is now my pastor. He pastored me then without knowing it. He was a "fit" gift from the Father as were my other two children. They were presented especially to me and to Jon. And though I often didn't feel like I was God's gift to them, when I look at their faces, I'm reminded that God created them for me, and He gives gifts that are fit for the one receiving them. They are good and perfect gifts, and I will spend the rest of my life thanking God for them and enjoying them.

To love children well is to mold them within the design. The way I see it, Proverbs 22:6 is a highly misunderstood verse. "Train up a child in the way he should go, even when he is old he will not depart from it." First, we mistakenly claim it as a promise. It's a proverb. It's wise to do what it says. When I was a young mother, I was taught the meaning of this verse this way: "Your child has a particular personality, a particular bent. You are to train that child within the 'bent'; don't try to make your child what she isn't, but teach her the truth and let her live it out her own way." In other words, don't try to shove your child into a mold. Fashionable, but I think it was fiction. To train up a child in the way she should go is to train her in the Way, a particular way. If you have to pick a mold, pick the Christian mold. Yes, your child has a unique personality; he also has a bent toward sin – like every human being. We want our children to come to faith early. We want them to learn to control their passions, not placate their passions to save their individuality. We want them to learn to kill their sins and to take their thoughts and emotions captive through repentance and faith, to grow up into Christians, militant for the kingdom of Christ. Our least concern is whether we've stepped on their last feeling.

What that old interpretation of Proverbs 22:6 was hinting at still has *some* merit. If the child God gave you is an introvert, and you wanted an extrovert, don't push for full blown extrovert. Teach your child ballast. Teach him to look people in the eyes, shake hands, be a man, but being an introvert is neither bad or sinful. Your son doesn't have to be a doctor or a football hero. If you wanted a boy and God gave you a girl, don't mold her into the boy you always wanted. Don't start reading vile pamphlets for gender transition. Receive the gift. Teach her to be a feminine, godly woman. Our focus should be righteousness. Train up your children in the way they should go – they should follow the way of the cross. The Christian way. Dying to self, not indulging self. Dying for others, not living solely for themselves. Loving others. Being hospitable and kind. Standing for truth. Mold them into what matters, and trust God for the fruit. God is completely in charge of their personality. Persevere to preserve their personalities, but insist on righteousness.

I belong to a somewhat continental reformed church now, but six years ago I was a committed Baptist. I can hang with both sides of the aisle, Christians all. At the risk of causing my Baptist friends to run screaming from the room, I would like to interject something here. For many years, I feared for my children. When they were little, I worried about screwing them up, not sharing the gospel at the right time in the right way. What if they never come to faith? When each of them prayed for salvation, I was there. And every time, I struggled. Was that real? What if I've simply taught them something that they don't really believe? What if their confession wasn't real? What if their baptism was too soon. I'm serious. I felt genuine angst. My husband and I expected obedience, but if they weren't Christians (and we were never sure), did they have power to obey? We became fruit inspectors looking for proof. I worried we might raise up good kids, but not godly kids. Do you suppose I had a problem with over-thinking things? When they became teenagers, each of them rebelled in their own ways. Many times, I would look back on their "salvation experiences" and rehearse all of my mistakes, taking the blame for their wanderings and repenting of my own distrust. When I saw all of my children returning to faith, I finally drew breath.

Not many years ago, Jon and I experienced a doctrinal shift. Our grown sons challenged us to question what we'd always been taught. They planted a church. We joined. This is where my Baptist friends might want to run from the room. I've not noticed the same kind of angst in the circles I'm in now. I don't have that angst for my grandchildren. Parents joyfully bring their children to worship. Children joyfully raise their hands and sing the doxology. We baptize our babies.[56] They are covenant members in the body of Christ and they know nothing else. The fear is removed. The level of trust that these children will be saved and experience a truly living faith is extremely high. They are moldable, not strong-willed stiff clay. What's the difference? A firm faith in the Lord to do as He promised:

> *They shall be my people, and I will be their God; and I will give them one heart and one way, that they may fear Me always,* ***for their own good and for the good of their children after them.*** *I will make an everlasting covenant with them that I will not turn away from them, to do them good; and I will put the fear of Me in their hearts so that they will not turn away from Me. Jeremiah 32:38-40*

[56] For my Baptist friends, we don't believe in baptismal regeneration (wet and elect), but we do believe in a real communion with the body of Christ for our children.

> *"As for Me, this is My covenant with them," says the LORD:* ***"My Spirit which is upon you and My words which I have put in your mouth shall not depart from your mouth, nor from the mouth of your offspring, nor from the mouth of your offspring's offspring,"*** *says the LORD, "from now and forever." Isaiah 59:21*

> *But the lovingkindness of the LORD is from everlasting to everlasting on those who fear Him, and* ***His righteousness to children's children,*** *to those who keep His covenant and remember His precepts to do them. Psalm 103:17-18*

> *Peter said to them, "Repent, and each of you be baptized in the name of Jesus Christ for the forgiveness of your sins; and you will receive the gift of the Holy Spirit.* ***For the promise is for you and your children*** *and for all who are far off, as many as the Lord our God will call to Himself. Acts 2:38-39*

> *But Jesus called for them, saying "****Permit the children to come to Me, and do not hinder them, for the kingdom of God belongs to such as these.****" Luke 18:16 (all bold mine)*

I would ask you to consider the way children are viewed in your congregation and what you've been taught and believe concerning their salvation. It makes a difference in the way we parent. Children of Christians are covenantally holy – this makes a world of difference in how we raise them in the faith. It makes a difference in our own faith.

To love children well means educating them. Charles Bridges wrote his commentary on the book of Proverbs over 175 years ago. His words are relevant even now:

> *Everything hangs on a child's training. Two paths beckon him. One path leads to ruin, the other to heaven. All training that is not based on the principles of the Bible must be harmful. To expand the mind without at the same time enlightening it is but to increase its power for evil. It would be far better to consign it to total ignorance, in that an uninstructed savage is less dangerous than a well-informed infidel… Yet the religious training of a child must not be the edge of a garment that can easily be trimmed off. It must be the pervading substance of his life. Pray for your child. Teach your child to pray. Instruct him from childhood in the holy Scriptures as the sole rule of faith and way to behave.*[57]

We need only look at the culture around us to know that public education does not meet this criterion. My children went to public school and survived. Barely. But is that what we are hoping for? Survival? We want our children to thrive in all aspects of their lives, but the foundation for that is a living faith. I encourage you to resolve to educate your children with intentionality, and to not just do as those before you have done. Pray about and consider good Christian schools or homeschooling. Base their training on the Bible. Expand *and* enlighten their minds. Catechize them. God truly can make a way for your child's best. We can't treat our children as if they were born only for this world. Our primary objective is a saved child with a living faith, not a satisfied child with a lukewarm faith. There is an eternity ahead of them. We are training them for the marathon, not the sprint. We need to jettison any thought that success means they must be like everyone else. We don't want our children keeping in step with the world.

> *Hear, O Israel: the LORD our God, the LORD is one. You shall love the LORD your God with all your heart and with all your soul and with all your might. And these words that*

---

[57] Charles Bridges, *Proverbs. The Crossway Classic Commentaries* (Illinois: Crossway Books, 2001).

I command you today shall be on your heart. You shall teach them diligently to your children, and shall talk of them when you sit in your house, and when you walk by the way, and when you lie down, and when you rise. You shall bind them as a sign on your hand, and they shall be as frontlets between your eyes. You shall write them on the doorposts of your house and on your gates. Deuteronomy 6:4-9

To love our children well demands discipline. Indulging the sins and whims of our children (just because it seems easier) is not loving. In 1846, Charles Bridges also wrote, "Far better that children should cry under healthful correction, than that parents should afterwards cry under the bitter fruit to themselves and children, of neglected discipline.[58] Can I get an amen? Many times, mothers cave to their children's sinful demands in order to maintain affection or approval. They don't want to risk not being liked by their children. Young mothers must remember that the goal is the salvation and nurture of their children's souls, not happiness or success. To discipline God's way is to show we love them and want His best for them.

A wise son makes a glad father, but a foolish son is a sorrow to his mother. Proverbs 10:1

Whoever spares the rod hates his son, but he who loves him is diligent to discipline him. Proverbs 13:24

A foolish son is a grief to his father and bitterness to her who bore him. Proverbs 17:25

Discipline your son, for there is hope; do not set your heart on putting him to death. Proverbs 19:18

---

[58] Ibid.

> *He who does violence to his father and chases away his mother is a son who brings shame and reproach. Proverbs 19:26*

> *Discipline your son, and he will give you rest; he will give delight to your heart. Proverbs 29:17*

Discipline done right is not bad. In fact, to not discipline is to set your heart on putting your child to death (Prov. 19:18). I despise the old adage, "Well, boys will be boys" or "children will be children." Uh huh. The truth is boys will be men. Girls will be women. Don't let your boys stay boys through a lack of attentive, intentional, biblical discipline. One of *my* grand-girls is going to marry one of *your* grandsons, and I don't want my grand-girls serving drinks and meals in the basement to Vinnie the Video Player. Boys need to be disciplined to walk uprightly and to work hard. They default to Neanderthal. Practical jokes aren't practical, and fart jokes aren't funny. Train them in true wit and wisdom. Train them to put others before themselves, to be loving and compassionate, strong, hardworking, creative, biblically literate, educated, disciplined men. Discipline your girls. Teach them that it's not okay to bat their eyelashes and work feminine wiles on dad or anyone else. It's called manipulation and it's sinful. Discipline them toward modesty, kindness, honesty, and chastity. Educate them well and teach them to be wise and strong in faith and love and in reason.

Be a Christian, mom.

Gift your children with a parent that is easy to honor.

> *Children, obey your parents in the LORD, for this is right. HONOR YOUR FATHER AND MOTHER (which is the first commandment with a promise), SO THAT IT MAY BE WELL WITH YOU, AND THAT YOU MAY LIVE LONG ON THE EARTH. Fathers, do no provoke*

your children to anger, but bring them up in the discipline and instruction of the Lord. Ephesians 6:1-4

Children, be obedient to your parents in all things, for this is well-pleasing to the Lord. Fathers, do not exasperate your children, so that they will not lose heart. Colossians 3:20-21

Since this book is written to women in God's church, I have not focused on the role of fathers. Suffice it to say, though, a husband's responsibility in marriage, in family, in church, and in the workplace is immense. Without Christ, a man can't even hope to achieve the ends for which he was created. God puts the primary emphasis of teaching and disciplining children on the father. As helpers, we are to come alongside him in those things, loving our children and setting an example for them to follow.

Children are already primed for tantrums. Parents don't need to add fodder. We are commanded as parents not to provoke them, exasperate them, or stir them up to anger. This requires that we control our own tempers. It's far too easy to crush the spirit of a child. As we parent, we should behold our heavenly Father, following His lead in parenting. My daughter-in-law does this particularly well. She smiles, keeps her voice low and even, and brings calm into the mix, yet her children do not doubt the authority she wields. She calls them to repentance and restitution quickly and kindly. Her children adore her and obey her. My other daughter-in-law disciplines with three rules in mind for obedience. Her children are to obey quickly, cheerfully, and thoroughly. Her home is set up like the garden with more "yeses" than "nos." It is ordered freedom. My daughter's home overflows with joy and kindness toward one another with an emphasis on serving one another. I've witnessed an easy giving between her two children, esteeming one another before themselves, and they are only ten and seven. These are things that cause a grandmother to long for do-overs. Do you want to be a parent your children will honor? Take advice from my girls. Obey your heavenly Father quickly, cheerfully, and thoroughly. Your Lord is a Lord of "Yes and amen." Repent and believe Him and see God smiling at you. Let's teach our children *and* ourselves that the way of the transgressor is hard, but the way of the Lord is life.

I'm an older woman with grown children. I look back often in regret and wish I had loved my children better. I wish I had stepped out of my selfish comfort and engaged them more in play. I wish I hadn't made rules willy-nilly and for my own convenience. I wish we had eaten more meals together instead of in shifts. I wish I had allowed them to teach me the art of silliness. I wish I had laughed more with them. I wish I had opened every single day with them singing and reading God's word. I wish I had prayed *with* them as much as I prayed *over* them. I wish we had danced even more than we did. I wish I had wielded more grace than justice, more compassion than fixes, more truth, more love, more encouragement, more hope. I wish I had given them so much more to honor. Don't be a wisher, young woman. Seize the day and love your children well, right now. Show them the rhythm of the Christian life. Repent and believe in front of them. Model joy. Be a Christian, mom.

Chapter 11

Submission is Our Superpower

In the same way, you wives, ***be submissive to your own husbands…***
1 Peter 3:1a

I'd like a dime for every "yeah, but…" I hear when submission is mentioned to a woman. It's always followed by "what if…" or "what about…" or "her husband…" or "my husband…" or "you just don't understand…"

Submission is the Christian way. It's not just a matter in marriage, though that is our focus here. There are other relationships that demand Christian submission. We are to submit to one another (Eph. 5:20-21), to church leaders who keep watch over our souls (Heb. 13:17), to human institutions (1 Pet. 2:13), to employers (1 Pet. 2:18), to elders (1 Pet. 5:5), and – of course and in all things – we submit to God (James 4:7). It's what we do. Well, until we get married and then we say, "yeah, but…"

Many ladies underestimate the safety of submission. We don't understand that submission is actually a gift to us, not a curse. Most tend to think hierarchy had to have come from the fall. How could God be a fan of inequality? But headship was part of the original design. Though Adam, Eve, and the serpent all experienced heavy consequences from the fall, the responsibility – the fall itself – fell on the shoulders of Adam. In the language of the Bible, Eve was deceived; Adam sinned.

No doubt things did get messy after the fall. This verse has messed with many a woman's head (pun intended): "To the woman He said, 'I will make your pains in childbearing very severe, with painful labor you will give birth to children. Your desire will be for your husband, and he will rule over you" (Gen. 3:16). Praise God there is no sin in heaven or else poor Eve would have a line of women outside her mansion rioting, fingers wagging and fists flailing. Don't blame her. We would have done the same thing. Our desire (our longing) will be for our husband, and he will rule (exercise dominion) over us. *This* is a result of the fall. It's a descriptor of slavery, not the model for marriage. How do we know?

Look with me to Gen. 4:7. Remember Cain and Abel? God said to Cain, "If you do what is right, will you not be accepted? But if you do not do what is right, sin is crouching at your door; it desires to have you, but you must rule over it." Look at the similarities between these two verses that use this word *desire*; they are crazy similar.

Your desire will be for your husband, and he will rule over you. Genesis 3:16

Sin…desires to have you, but you must rule over it. Genesis 4:7

God was saying to Cain, "Sin wants to overpower you. It's right there, crouching like a lion waiting to pounce and devour. It wants to defeat you and rule over you, make you it's slave." If we take this back to Gen. 3:16, we can see the same sinful desire in women. "When sin has the upper hand in woman, she will desire to overpower or subdue or exploit man. And when sin has the upper hand in man, he will respond in like manner and with strength subdue her, or rule over her."[59]

John Piper, discussing biblical manhood and womanhood, reminds us that when God created us in His image, male and female, it does imply an equality of a kind. He gives six ways: equality of personhood, equality of dignity (equally honored as humans in God's image), equality in mutual respect (equally zealous to respect one another), equally harmonious (peaceful cooperation between men and women), equal in complementarity (*differences* should be equally affirmed and valued, highlighting each other's

[59] John Piper, *Manhood and Womanhood – Conflict and Confusion After the Fall.* DesiringGod.org, May 21, 1989.

unique qualities), and finally equal in unified destiny (we are all fellow heirs of the grace of life). But in our sin, Genesis 3:16 is our default as women. Sometimes we just want our way, our rights. We want to rule over him.

Adam and Eve fell. From what? If what we've just seen was part of the curse, then what is the blessing? The blessing is God designed order. The husband is the head of the wife as Christ is head of the church. As Christians, we get to live out the better scenario: What if Adam and Eve had obeyed in the garden? The second Adam, Jesus Christ, calls us to the original design in marriage. His desire is to show forth the original blueprint. Consequently, *headship* is not a part of the curse; instead, it is the plan. It is good. And submission is a part of headship.

That's Not Submission

Before we talk about what true submission to our husbands looks like, let's take a look at what it is not.[60]

When we submit, we don't agree on everything. Frankly, if we agreed with our spouses on everything, we would be married to ourselves. That's a horror to me. And what if a husband is an unbeliever? We certainly can't agree with an unbelieving spouse on everything and remain faithful to Jesus. We have minds. We can discern if something is right or true. God never intended for us to be cookie-cutter images of our husbands. We are his crown.

With the above in mind, remember that ***submission does not mean we have to have permission for everything we do.*** Christ designed us to be helpers who think independently of our husbands. Our opinions are worth something. Jon listens to what I have to say and respects my opinions. He may not always choose my way, but He often does. I don't need to be right all the time. Submission doesn't mean we refuse to influence our husbands. It

[60] These submission "nots" are from John Piper's "This Momentary Marriage," a wealth of marriage wisdom that I highly recommend to you. I've rephrased them a little, but they are his, not mine.

does mean we refuse to manipulate them. Not only is manipulation sinful; it just doesn't work.

True submission never puts what a husband wants over what Christ wants. Whenever we must choose between them, and we might, we must choose Christ. We can show our husbands our sadness when they choose contrary to God's way, but with humility of mind, we can state that we are going to follow God. Though in doing this, we have to remember our own fallibility. Often, we can sinfully convince ourselves that our own desires are God's ways when they aren't. We can't let our own self-righteousness side against our husbands and against God. I am not advocating standing against your husband in every decision he makes if you disagree. Our hubris is as bad as theirs. Poor leadership and bad decisions are not always sinful decisions. I am advocating standing against blatantly sinful decisions. For example, if a husband decides it would suit his marriage to bring pornography into the bedroom, "no" is the right decision. Women aren't obliged to join their husbands in theft, lies, idolatry, or any kind of sin or rebellion against God. Submitting to God first trains us to know how to submit to our husbands.

Submission doesn't mean that all of our spiritual knowledge and strength comes from our husbands. We must prove ourselves to be women of the word and develop our hope in Christ. Many husbands have a wealth of spiritual knowledge and truth to impart to their wives, and I say "yes and amen" to women who listen to them and learn from them. But I truly believe women must learn to feed themselves from the word of God and be trained by others in the church. Before my husband was a Christian, I got up every Sunday morning, dressed my little girl, and we went to church. Each Sunday I asked my husband, "Would you like to come with us?" Each Sunday he said no. This went on for quite some time. Finally, one Sunday I just didn't bother to ask. He stopped me. "Aren't you going to ask me to church?" He went that day. He told me later that he thought I had given up on him. Back then, my spiritual strength came from the Lord and His church. God was gracious to change my husband's heart. My spiritual knowledge and strength is still found in Christ, but now, it often comes through my husband. Quiet faithfulness speaks volumes, invokes holy influence, and reaps gracious blessings.

Submission Defined

What is submission? It is a military term. It means to come under authority in an orderly fashion. My father was the highest rank he could achieve as a non-commissioned officer in the Air Force. He still had to stop and salute my best friend's dad who was a Colonel.[61] He respected and obeyed the officers above him, just as the lower ranked NCO's respected and obeyed him. When these guys got together for poker and a beer, all the ranks were put in their pockets. They were just guys who liked cards and Coors. Submission to our husbands is similar. We respect and obey the office of husband and his headship. If you are chafing under this fact, have you considered Jesus?

The emphasis in Ephesians 5:22-33 is on marriage as a model and picture of Christ and His church. The husband is to love his wife as Christ loved the church and gave Himself up for her. The wife is to be subject to her husband as to the Lord, the way the church is subject to Christ. We know that a wife's submission is voluntary, a willful choice to lay aside her own will and to choose her husband's will. In our culture, this looks as though we women got shafted. This is not the case. Consider Christ.

> *Jesus said to them, "My food is to do the will of Him who sent Me, and to accomplish His work." John 4:34*

> *I can do nothing on My own initiative. As I hear, I judge; and My judgment is just, because I do not seek My own will, but the will of Him who sent Me. John 5:30*

[61] His name was Colonel Sanders. I always found that amusing and expected fried chicken when I went to her home.

> *For I have come down from heaven, not to do My own will, but the will of Him who sent Me. John 6:38*
>
> *And He who sent Me is with Me; He has not left Me alone, for I always do the things that are pleasing to Him. John 8:29*
>
> *I delight to do Your will, O my God; Your Law is within my heart. Ps. 40:8*
>
> *Have this attitude in yourselves which was also in Christ Jesus, who, although He existed in the form of God, did not regard equality with God a thing to be grasped, but emptied Himself, taking the form of a bond-servant, and being made in the likeness of men. Being found in appearance as a man, He humbled Himself by becoming obedient to the point of death, even death on a cross. For this reason also, God highly exalted Him, and bestowed on Him the name which is above every name, so that at the name of Jesus EVERY KNEE WILL BOW, of those who are in heaven and on earth and under the earth, and that every tongue will confess that Jesus Christ is Lord, to the glory of God the Father. Philippians 2:5-11*

If Jesus, who is God, who has all power and authority given to Him, who brought you in and can take you out, willingly submitted to the will of His Father and did not grasp for the real equality that was His, who are we to balk at His command to us to submit to our husbands as to Him? It's rather arrogant to think that we could have our independence and not make a mess of it. We should throw our hands up and volunteer to submit. Be joyful about it. We get to show forth the glory of Christ and His bride. As Kathy Keller says, you get to "play the Jesus role too."[62]

[62] Timothy Keller with Kathy Keller. *The Meaning of Marriage* (New York: Dutton, 2011).

Piper also gives us a wonderful pared down definition of submission: it is "the divine calling of a wife to honor and affirm her husband's leadership and help carry it through according to her gifts."[63] This definition fits us as helpers. Submission "is not absolute surrender of her will. Rather, we speak of her disposition to yield to her husband's guidance and her inclination to follow his leadership. Christ is her absolute authority, not the husband. She submits out of reverence for Christ (Eph. 5:21). The supreme authority of Christ qualifies the authority of her husband. She should never follow her husband into sin."[64] We think to submit to someone is to surrender control. Of course that would be scary! But when we resist submission, we are showing disdain for God's authority. Submission is to be a free, voluntary, joyful service to Christ Himself, with the aim of honoring and affirming the husband God has ordained to lead.

I know some women who submit so easily that I've often wondered if they aren't possessed of some special gene that fell out of my DNA. Then I know others who most definitely are "sitting on the outside, but *standing* on the inside." I also know other women who ignore the command altogether, calling it outdated and an assault on their rights. We can all be guilty of an internal rebellious sass whether we admit it or act upon it. There are times we certainly do want to say, "You're not the boss of me." All of this internal falderal can come from weariness, from being over-ruled or bullied, from pride, rebellion or entitlement. I'm not minimizing the struggle. The fight against ourselves is real. What does internal sass look like? Are you a cabinet slammer? Do you stay offended over bad decisions that you had no part in making?[65] Do you internally call your husband a fool? Do you minor in nagging? Do you withhold respect? Do you lock the bedroom "safe" and change the combination? Do you manipulate and try to lead from behind thinking, "I'm happy to submit after he agrees with me." Do you internally

[63] John Piper, *This Momentary Marriage: A Parable of Permanenece* (Wheaton, IL: Crossway Books, 2009).

[64] John Piper and Wayne Grudem, *Recovering Biblical Manhood and Womanhood* (Wheaton, IL: Crossway Books, 1991).

[65] Just so you know, it is as much a sin to stay offended as it is to offend. Just saying.

whine, complain, grumble or talk him down in your mind? To others? Do you rehearse your husband's sins more than confessing your own?

Fearless Submission

Sometimes my emotional lines get tangled, and I'm surprised at my own defensiveness on this subject. I had a discussion with my eldest son about this, not only in the context of marriage, but in the context of church leadership. To use my husband's description of me, I "bowed up." For the most part, I agreed with my son, but I found myself getting more and more defensive to the point that I needed a good deflating. It soon became evident to me that submission and authority really aren't the issue for most of us – or maybe I should just speak for myself. I think the root is more likely fear: fear of authority, fear of correction, fear of failure, fear of being bullied and abused, fear of being minimalized, fear of being unprotected and not cared for, fear of being forgotten, unimportant, mediocre. We don't have the promise that every authority that we are called to submit to has our best interest in mind. We can't be certain they won't be heavy-handed and arrogant, that we won't be lied to or betrayed. We can't be certain that this particular authority doesn't have a dark side.

Actually, and this is hard to swallow, submission is the way *out* of fear.

> *In the same way, you wives, be submissive to your own husbands so that even if any of them are disobedient to the word, they may be won without a word by the behavior of their wives, as they observe your chaste and respectful behavior. Your adornment must not be merely external - braiding the hair, and wearing gold jewelry, or putting on dresses; but let it be the hidden person of the heart with the imperishable quality of a gentle and quiet spirit, which is precious in the sight of God. For in this way in former times the holy women also, who hoped in God, used to adorn themselves, being submissive to their own husbands; just as Sarah obeyed Abraham, calling*

> *him lord, and you have become her children if you do what is right without being frightened by any fear. You husbands in the same way, live with your wives in an understanding way, as with someone weaker, since she is a woman; and show her honor as a fellow heir of the grace of life, so that your prayers will not be hindered. 1 Peter 3:1-7*

God doesn't promise us that the authorities over us will always be just, kind, loving, or even thrifty and wise. Those that lead us in the church are saved sinners. Those that lead us in our workplaces may not even be Christians. Our brothers and sisters in Christ are being sanctified just like you and me. We can be married to knuckleheads (and so might our husbands), or as Peter just told us, many women are married to husbands who "do not obey the word" and who don't show their wives honor or live with them in "an understanding way." This is why we fear. A perfectly just, kind, loving, understanding, honoring, thrifty, wise, godly person would be a joy to submit to, right? You would think so. Every Christian has a perfect "head," Jesus, yet we don't submit perfectly to Him. This is why we are commanded to submit in a specific way: as to the Lord.

> *Wives, be subject to your own husbands, as to the Lord. Ephesians 5:22*

> *Wives, be subject to your husbands, as is fitting in the Lord. Colossians 3:18*

> *But as the church is subject to Christ, so also the wives ought to be to their husbands in everything. Ephesians 5:24*

As to the Lord, as is fitting in the Lord, in everything. Consider Jesus. This is how we tame our fears. We submit to the perfect authority first. And we submit to the imperfect authority as is fitting in the Lord. 1 Peter 3:5-6 gives us some hints regarding a Christian woman's way of fearless submission.

> *For in this way in former times the holy women also, who hoped in God, used to adorn themselves, being submissive to their own husbands; just as Sarah obeyed Abraham, calling him lord, and you have become her children if you do what is right without being frightened by any fear."*

First, look where these holy women placed their hope. It wasn't placed in their husbands. (Note: Single women, your hope is in God, not in apprehending a husband.) We are also not to put our hope in ourselves, what we do, what we don't do, or in our friends. God wants women to put their hope in Him first. Hope in Christ begets right submission.

What does it mean to *hope in God?* One of my favorite Psalms is Psalm 42. I regularly wear it out. The common refrain in it is: "Why are you in despair, O my soul? And why have you become disturbed within Me? Hope in God..." Why hope in Him? Because "I shall again praise Him for the help of His presence" (Ps. 42:5). He will help me. "I shall yet praise Him, the help of my countenance and my God" (Ps. 42:1). He will help me and He is my God. That's enough. We can trust Him to care for us even when others fail to do so. "The LORD will command His lovingkindness in the daytime; and His song will be with me in the night, a prayer to the God of my life" (Ps. 42:8). He is more than enough. This requires faith. Sometimes our needs feel bigger than we believe our God is. Hope, my sister. Believe God.

A woman who hopes in God trusts in the sovereignty of God. "Strength and dignity are her clothing and she smiles at the future" (Proverbs 31:25). We can't look into tomorrow; God hasn't even promised us one. But if there is one, He has already been there. He has prepared a work for you to do in advance of your arrival. He has already provided everything you need for life and godliness in Christ. A Christian who hopes simply trusts and shows up for duty. Strength and dignity are a hopeful woman's adornment.

So is submission. "The holy women who hoped in God used to adorn themselves, by submitting to their own husbands..." When we know the word of God, the promises of God, and we are transformed by that word, becoming what it teaches, we can bow to whatever God allows in our lives because we trust His goodness. Not only that He is good, but that He is good to us. Our inner life is adorned with the fruit of the Spirit, the virtues of Christ Himself, and our hope is tangible, right in front of us, by the word of God and the presence of Christ. We submit to our husbands from this place, and fear has to flee. We become fearless. We are "not frightened by any fear."

Several years ago, my husband was working for a printing plant near us. He had started working from home. One morning, he was called into the main office. About three hours later, he came back home and numbly said, "I've been let go." We just stared at one another. Then he said, "I don't know what to do." Left to myself, worry would have overtaken me. But I immediately prayed, "Lord, what do I say?" I opened my mouth and out came, "Well, we can take a walk." We put on our shoes and took a silent pilgrimage through the neighborhood. A long one. I broke the silence with, "God is sovereign. This must be the plan. If this is the plan, then it's good. Let's just start there." And we did. We trusted God. I trusted God in my husband. Three months later, he took a job taking home a third less in pay. God took care of us. God blessed him. He's still working for the same company. God is good to us.

Cowardice has no place in the life of a Christian woman. Frankly, I've learned in my almost forty years of marriage, being *unsubmissive* is easy, and it is cowardly. It's gutsy to submit. We gain our strength and dignity clothes through just this kind of obedience. It takes a strong woman, a woman dependent upon the Holy Spirit, a woman willing to lay down her life, a woman willing to repent of her own tendency toward self-protection, a woman who volunteers to trust and follow Christ by following the imperfect man who is leading her, to submit rightly. Submission dispels cowardice. Faith is not fearlessness; faith is trusting God in spite of fear. To submit is a simple declaration that our God is trustworthy.

Me? Submit? But…

I'm not naïve. I'm aware of the different situations women face, the different kinds of men they are married to, and the different states of life they are living in. In my sphere alone, I'm aware of a single woman who is struggling in a dating relationship and chafing under the authority of her church elders; a widow that wishes she had someone in authority over her – someone who would actually make decisions for her; a woman married to a Christian knucklehead who won't submit to the word of God in ruling his household and using their finances wisely; a woman married to a so-called Christian man who beats her on a regular basis; a woman married to a misogynistic bully who treats her like he bought her from a mail-order-bride magazine; a woman who believes her husband is weak and cowardly and wishes he would lead with more strength; a woman with a husband who desires to love her but who she pushes around with her tyrannical snark and nagging; a woman that has completely checked her mind at the marriage altar while her husband makes foolish decisions without a word from her; and many women who are submitting rightly to imperfect men who love them, love their children, follow Christ, and desire the best for their wives – the envied wives. Recognizing this, I would like to take a moment to address the subject of submission and its relevance for women in abusive marriages. Remember, as Christians, male and female, we are all subject to Christ first. We are all subject to other Christians. We are all subject to our local church leadership. We are all subject to our local, state, and federal authorities. And of course, these are not absolute authorities. Only Christ gets to hold that position.

Christian husbands who abuse their wives are, first of all, disobeying God. Christ does not beat His bride. Husbands should not beat their wives. Husbands should not berate and torment, threaten or bully their wives. Women who are intimidated this way are not expected to submit to their peril. They can lovingly submit by calling upon the other authorities to whom they submit, namely, their church elders and the local police. If a woman's elders are worth their salt, they can be her first form of shelter and line of defense. They can find her (and her children if she has any) a safe place. They can discipline her husband and call him to repentance. They can offer counsel and/or find them long-term counseling. If there are witnesses to the abuse, they can, if necessary, excommunicate an unrepentant husband. A woman can also freely call the police if she (or her children) is in danger. These actions are not contrary to her call to submit to her husband. In fact, these authorities are placed over her for her good, and it is an act of submission to avail herself of their care. It takes great courage and humility to deny self-protection and lies so as to place ourselves in the care of God-ordained authorities. Husbands are called to be the protectors of their families, not the main threat to their safety. Wives are under no obligation to protect the façade of a happy home in the name of submission, denying the demoralization, scandal, and destruction that are behind closed doors. God's call to all Christians is to live in truth.

Take a look at Abigail in 1 Samuel 25. The Scripture describes her as "intelligent and beautiful" and then describes her husband, Nabal (which means "fool"), as "harsh and evil in his dealings." David and his men were in need of supplies and Nabal refused to help them. David was furious and was on his way to destroy Nabal's household. Abigail dismissed Nabal's will and interceded, even taking the blame. She pleaded with David, being honest about Nabal's character, calling him worthless and saying, "As his name says, so he is."[66] She brought supplies to David and begged him to stay his hand against her family and servants and to ignore her foolish husband. David did as she requested. The next morning, after Nabal had sobered up, she told what she had done. The Bible says Nabal's "heart died within him so that he became as a stone." Then we are told that ten days later, "The Lord struck Nabal, and he died." After Nabal died, Abigail got a message from David with a marriage proposal. The King takes care of His faithful. He will take care of you if you are married to a Nabal.

---

[66] I call your attention to this verse in light of our chapter on slander. Abigail told the truth about her husband. It wasn't good for his reputation, but it wasn't slander. Nabal really was a fool.

We can now look back at 1 Peter 3:1-2 again, "In the same way, you wives, be subject to your own husbands so that *even if any of them are disobedient to the word,* they may be won over without a word by the behavior of their wives, as they observe your pure and respectful behavior." The word *disobedient* means literally "to refuse to believe or to withhold belief." It means to not allow oneself to be persuaded. Peter is speaking here of an unbelieving husband. This could be a Christian man that turns away and refuses to believe God, or a husband who is in total unbelief. For either, the call for the woman is the same. She is to be subject to him for the purpose of winning him. In other words, believe and act as though this is an opportunity to display Christ. Her hope is not in whether her husband turns from sin and turns to God; her hope is in Christ who is her ultimate husband.

Douglas Wilson posted an article entitled *Open Letter to a Trapped Wife*[67] on his blog site, *Blog and Mablog*. In it, he excellently exhorts women who are in these kinds of relationships:

> *If a godly wife is dealing with an ungodly and disobedient husband, and she is submissive in the way that Peter describes then she is actively bringing everything to a head. Either he will be shamed by her courtesy, and submit to the Word, becoming obedient to it, or he will leave, or make the situation intolerable. She is not a doormat here – she wins him. She, by her reverent and chaste behavior, wins through. Either he submits to Christ, in which case she has won her husband, or he reacts violently to her reverent and chaste behavior. When this latter situation is unfolding, many wives believe that they are doing something wrong because the anger of their husband is apparently getting worse. But a fish being hauled in does most of its thrashing right beside the boat. The husband's increased anger is a sign that he is getting to a break point. He is converted, or he ditches, or he makes home an impossible place to be. If the former, the*

[67] Douglas Wilson. *Open Letter to a Trapped Wife*. Dougwils.com (https://dougwils.com/books-and-culture/s7-engaging-the-culture/open-letter-to-a-trapped-wife.html).

> *problem is solved. If he leaves, the problem is solved. If he makes life in the home unlivable because of her reverent and chaste behavior, then she can leave with a clean conscience. Having left, she is prepared to cooperate fully with the elders when they seek to bring about a reconciliation. But that reconciliation will not occur unless there is repentance. Reconciliation is to be on God's terms, not hers, and certainly not his. Reconciliation is not the same thing as the fight blowing over, or the husband calming down just a bit.*

You see, ladies, submission is a gift from the Lord. He lifts our faces to His, and turns us away from our self-sufficiency. He empowers us in any situation to obey him, to submit first to Him, and then to our husbands. In this way, it truly is our superpower. We are supernaturally empowered by the Holy Spirit to repent of our own wants and schemes, and to depend on Christ and His word. A truly submissive wife has great influence. She can win her husband to Christ. She can sharpen her husband in Christ. Submission doesn't make you less. It makes you more… more secure, more lovely, more glorious, more fit for your husband and for heaven. Consider Jesus and His own submission to His Father. We are in great company. Older women, teach younger women to submit to their own husbands. Teach them not to neglect their superpower.

Chapter 12

Slavery or Sensibility

> *Older women likewise are to be reverent in their behavior, not malicious gossips* ***nor enslaved to much wine****, teaching what is good, so that they may encourage the young women to love their husbands, to love their children,* ***to be sensible...***
>
> *Titus 2:3-5a*

On what do you depend to be okay? I've encountered all types of women with all types of vices, addictions, obsessions, compulsions, and well, quirks. I've been one of those and still struggle with a few hitchhiking hang-ups that want to hang on. Oh, if I could only tell you that I've got the godly woman gig going on perfectly, but then there are too many witnesses to the contrary. And God hates liars.

Older women are admonished not be enslaved to much wine. Later, we're told to train younger women to be sensible (or sober-minded). These two attributes are conjoined. We can't talk about *not being* something without talking about *being* something. To not be enslaved and to be sensible are sides of the same coin.

Be Sober

Sobriety is an under-valued virtue to many of us unless one is an alcoholic or grew up around one. Paul is literally instructing Titus to pass on to these older Christian women: don't be a "drunkardess." Although Paul could be stating just that, I don't think it's wrong for us to think in terms of having a sober mind as well. We are not to let wine (or alcohol in general), passions, emotions, or lusts have excessive influence on our behavior or decisions. We are to be wise, circumspect, judicious, cautious, prudent and discerning.[68] It's a little difficult to be these if we're sloshed or stoned, right? The Bible tells us in Ephesians 5:18, "Do not get drunk with wine, for that is debauchery, but be filled with the Spirit." Debauchery is intemperance. It is to overindulge in sensual pleasures. Wine makes the heart of man glad; too much of it creates a fool. Consider this from the book of Proverbs:

> *Who has woe? Who has sorrow? Who has contentions? Who has complaining? Who has wounds without cause? Who has redness of eyes? Those who linger long over wine, those who go to taste mixed wine. Do not look on the wine when it is red, when it sparkles in the cup, when it goes down smoothly; at the last it bites like a serpent and stings like a viper. Your eyes will see strange things and your mind will utter perverse things. And you will be like one who lies down in the middle of the sea, or like one who lies down on the top of a mast. "They struck me, but I did not become ill; They beat me, but I did not know it. When shall I awake? I will seek another drink."*
> *Proverbs 23:29-35*

Too much wine and this dude's got issues! And yet when he wakes, the next drink is on his mind. Does this sound like anyone you've known? I've known quite a few drunkards. I lived with one from toddler to well past teen. We all preferred "alcoholic" because it made it sound like it wasn't my dad's fault. We could blame everything on the disease. After over thirty years of the disease, it was cured after a car accident, a tongue lashing, a heavy dose of shame, and some self-control. My dad came to his senses. He returned to Jesus a few years later.

[68] Could I buy another adjective?

I'm passionate about the subject of alcohol and its use. My father was a career drunk throughout my entire youth. He returned from Korea with a problem when I was four. That problem progressively grew into everyone's problem. It wreaked havoc on our family, sometimes like a hurricane, but mostly like a slow-acting poison. Dad was seldom sober, but he was high functioning. He held a job, but he also held a couple of harlots as well as the responsibility for some crazy financial hijinks. I'm not dishonoring his memory; just being honest. He was truly flawed, and he truly lost the ability to think soberly about what his drinking was doing to the people who loved him most. The Bible is true when it says "wine is a mocker, strong drink a brawler, and whoever is led astray by it is not wise" (Prov. 20:1). My family was an eyewitness to this truth. Parenting under the influence does shameful damage to children and spouses. We have a responsibility to the "watchers." I have memories, as a five-year-old, of my father with a pail of Stag Beer. That was the perfect name for what it did to him. He was staggering back to the car. Children see. And just because our children are grown and out of the home, doesn't mean the gin is free to flow like a flashflood. Marriages can be poisoned and broken by it.

Our family was saved from this familial alcohol poisoning when my father was well into retirement. After some well-placed divine circumstances and a heart change, my father mellowed, quit using alcohol to anesthetize whatever he had been hiding for all of those years, and joined the world around him. To God be the glory! Yet the damage lingers sometimes, doesn't it.

I'm not an abolitionist. I like real wine on Sunday with the bread. I like wine on Sunday, period. I like a finely made amaretto sour and a good Italian cranappletini. Heck, my husband is a home beer brewer who regularly reminds me what Benjamin Franklin said: "Beer is proof that God loves us and wants us to be happy." Ben also said, "In wine there is wisdom, in beer there is freedom, in water there is bacteria." Therefore, my friend, I can wholeheartedly agree with Paul who said to Timothy, "No longer drink water exclusively, but use a little wine for the sake of your stomach and your frequent ailments." Grape juice doesn't cut it. Yes, and amen.

Alcohol, though, isn't the only misused drug. Our community, as well as communities all over our nation, has an opioid and heroine epidemic that is ravaging households. Prescription drugs and marijuana use are off the charts. We've taught ourselves that pain isn't allowed. We don't know how to suffer and to suffer well, so we find ways to make sure we don't suffer at all. Anesthetics abound; we simply don't think we are sucking the gas. Think about what we do to *not* think. When we are overwhelmed, anxious, hurt, angry, shamed, confused, at our leisure or bored, we choose our favorite comforters. Drugs, alcohol, cutting, starving ourselves, gluttony, smoking, sugar, books, movies, social media, television, gaming, sex, shopping, relationships, phones, and the list goes on and on. Take your pick, or better yet, don't. It's not that all of these things are sins. Obviously, they aren't. Good things are still good; it's just our inordinate or unruly desires ruin the fun and make us slaves to our loves.

The word *enslaved* in Titus 2:3 gives us a clue. It's a word that means to bind yourself to something or someone. The King James Version says "given to much wine." That version gives us the gist of the word used here: As Christians, we don't fall into slavery, we give ourselves over to it. This verse is warning us about addiction. Older women, and I realize I am stretching this past wine and alcohol, are not to be enslaved to anything. What we need is found in Titus 2:5 – sensibility. And it's what we teach younger women.

Sensibility

Though the Bible version that I prefer uses *sensible*, this is the same virtue we've previously looked at translated *sound mind*. The other aspect we need to touch on is self-control. Temperance, the balance of our passions, results when we are self-controlled. Self-control is a misunderstood virtue today. We think it's all about telling ourselves "no." It can be, but more importantly, to be self-controlled is to be disciplined in our freedom, in our "yeses." Let's look at what life looks like without it.

"Like a city that is broken into and without walls is a man who has no control over his spirit" (Prov. 25:28). This language is a little foreign to us.

Our city isn't fortified by walls. But walls (think Bible times) were meant for security and defense. To have a breach in the wall was to be vulnerable. A city surrounded by rubble rather than walls was defenseless, overrun by its enemies.

Think of your mind (or heart, the seat of your emotions) as a city. Self-control, given and empowered by the Holy Spirit, is the wall that surrounds it. Self-control restrains our passions and desires. It helps us walk discreetly, soberly, and moderately. 1 Corinthians 6:12 is the voice of self-control speaking to us: "All things are lawful for me, but not all things are profitable. All things are lawful for me, but I will not be mastered by anything." We want the residents of this city (our mind) to experience freedom, but we have to be discriminating. Our thoughts, inclinations, passions, emotions… these must all prove to be good tenants. Sinful squatters are not allowed to live rent free in our heads.

Teaching younger women self-control is more about teaching them to live by grace through faith, about teaching sin-killing and living by faith. Paul tells the Colossians that he toils to bring believers to maturity in Christ, but he does it "striving according to His (the Holy Spirit's) power, which mightily works within me" (Col. 1:29). There's a conundrum. Self-control is a gift, produced by the power of Christ in us, made efficient by the Spirit, but we work it out in our day-to-day.

Sin Killing

For Christians, self-control is an equally needed virtue, not gender or age specific. The term itself implies some sort of battle. Something must be mastered by someone. The world's self-control campaign is a *Nike* campaign: "Just say no" if you want to stop. Behave if you have to. They think in terms of "putting on the brakes." Christians have another way. Our self-control is not defined as "control yourself"; our self-control is defined more as "Kill the interloper; serve a new master." Inordinate passions that are trying to squat within us are not just ushered to the door, they are ushered to the gallows. Self-control is meant to be fierce against its foes. Jesus describes this fierceness in Matthew 5:29-30:

> *If your right eye makes you stumble, tear it out and throw it from you; for it is better for you to lose one of the parts of your body, than for your whole body to be thrown into hell. If your right hand makes you stumble, cut if off and throw it from you; for it is better for you to lose one of the parts of your body, than for your whole body to go into hell.*

Paul put it this way: "For if you live according to the flesh, you will die, but if by the Spirit you put to death the deeds of the body, you will live" (Ro. 8:13). Desires are God-given. Inordinate desires, desires run amuck and acted upon, are sins. Women, we are to be ruthless when we deal with unruly or out of control desires, immoral thoughts, and the like. We can't give them time to make a defense for themselves. We cut them off. It's the only admissible murder. We kill what Christ has already killed.

> *Therefore do not let sin reign in your mortal body so that you obey its lusts, and do not go on presenting the members of your body to sin as instruments of unrighteousness; but present yourselves to God as those alive from the dead, and your members as instruments of righteousness to God. For sin shall not be master over you, for you are not under law but under grace. Romans 6:12-14*

For all of us, but particularly women, we have to remember that Christ is far better than anything we could manufacture for our own pleasure. He's not just better when our needs are more than we can manage. He is *always* the better choice. His will or His pleasure will satisfy us. In His presence is fullness of joy. At His right hand are pleasures forevermore (Ps. 16:11). In those moments when we agonize with emotions, thoughts, and desires, for whatever reason – maybe we feel lonely, unloved, empty, bored, hungry, discontented, angry, wounded, abandoned, betrayed, frustrated, numb, distracted, or maybe we just plain want what we want when we want it – we must believe that Jesus is more desirable than anything we would choose to satisfy ourselves. We must believe that we are united with Him in His death, burial, and resurrection and that every sin we come up against has been killed in Christ, and therefore we can trust that our lust is no match for His righteousness. We can put on self-control by faith, and the Holy Spirit will empower us to choose rightly. When our flesh offers the smorgasbord of substitutes – "try television, fantasizing, social networks, mommy porn, books, drinking, drugs, sleeping, eating, working harder, shopping, spending, exercise, partying, gaming," you name it – we can say by faith in Christ, "No, Jesus is better."

A few chapters ago, I alluded to some strongholds in my thoughts and imagination. I showed a progression of saying no, then NO, then "You're not the boss of me" until I was finally free. It was a slow progression and it wasn't a straight line. It looked more like climbing a mountain with switchbacks. Further up, but down and across every now and then. Winning the battle over sin with extremely deep roots takes time. It takes falling down and getting up. Repent. Believe. Repent. Believe. That particular battle has taught me to set up Ebenezer stones along the way.

> *Then Samuel took a stone and set it between Mizpah and Shen, and named it Ebenezer, saying, "Thus far the LORD has helped us." 1 Samuel 7:12*

For every battle with my flesh that I won, I would give thanks to the LORD and say out loud, "Thus far the LORD has helped me." I would fail the next one and confess to the LORD. I would repent and thank Him for His forgiveness and for His help the next time. Pretty soon the time between my failures got longer and longer, until finally, I would almost laugh when the temptation to indulge my imagination came. "Thus far the LORD has helped me… I don't need that anymore." In my journals, I would call these "EDeniser" stones. My memorials to the faithfulness of God my

Help, and my gratitude for the fruit of self-control. Apart from Him, I was impotent to break free. He is our wisdom, righteousness, sanctification and redemption. He is the sin slayer, and we need only confess our dependence upon Him, boasting in His sufficiency, relying upon all He has done for us, and acting upon the truth of who we really are: new, no longer slaves to sin, but indeed slaves to righteousness.

Without self-control, small seeds of sin are left unattended. Starting as unchecked desires, they become inordinate, unsatisfied desires. Placated enough, they become sins, then habits, then addictions, then strongholds. Now instead of a wall of self-control protecting our hearts, we have a hedge of brambles that has walled up our heart and made it a slave to its own passions. A self-controlled woman guards her heart through repentance, pulling the seedlings and young weeds out by the roots before they take over the heart's affections. Self-control is not really about bringing our passions under our own control, but about making them bow to Christ. We can indulge our desires to a point and still not sin, but self-control calls us to limit our freedom for our good and God's pleasure. Our pleasures bow to God's good and perfect will.

Beautiful Slaves

In the words of Bob Dylan, "Well, it may be the devil or it may be the Lord but you're gonna have to serve somebody." He wasn't lying.

> *Do you not know that when you present yourselves to someone as slaves for obedience, you are slaves of the one whom you obey, either of sin resulting in death, or of obedience resulting in righteousness? But thanks be to God that though you were slaves of sin, you became obedient from the heart to that form of teaching to which you were committed, and having been freed from sin, you became slaves of righteousness. Romans 6:16-18*

> *But now having been freed from sin and enslaved to God, you derive your benefit, resulting in sanctification, and the outcome, eternal life. Romans 6:22*

Christians are enslaved to Christ. We are slaves to righteousness. Self-control chooses the pleasure of the King over our own carnal pleasures. It is the guardian of our hearts.

Self-control (or sensibility) is also our adornment. 1 Timothy 2:9-10 translates self-control (sensible) as *discreet*. "Likewise I want women to adorn themselves with proper clothing, modestly and *discreetly*, not with braided hair and gold or pearls or costly garments, but rather by means of good works, as is proper for women making a claim to godliness." Many women look at this verse and think, "Isn't that beautiful? Modesty and self-control are more beautiful than a good hairstyle, gold, pearls and a ballgown." True, but I would rather think of this new apparel as beautifully utilitarian, like Eowyn's apparel in the movie *The Lord of the Rings: The Return of the King*. It's beauty that is fit for battle and battles sin to the death. "I AM NO MAN," as she throws her helmet to the ground and reveals her tresses. Epic. This is self-control that takes no prisoners, beautifies the actual wielder of the sword (the Holy Spirit), and cuts off the head of every enemy that would claim to be greater than Christ.

Older women must exemplify this and train young women around them to identify unruly desires, emotions, and thoughts, and then to stand firm in all that Christ has done, to believe that we are united to Him in His death and life, and that by faith and by the Spirit, we can force those lusts, emotions and thoughts to bow to the sword of Christ and lay their crushed heads on the block. They must submit to His rule. Self-control is our friend; it's the virtue that holds hands with repentance and faith to cut off the head of every sin that sets itself up against the better Christ. Be a woman who stands on God's battlefield and sees it littered with the corpses of her own lusts. Be sensible. Be sober. Be self-controlled. Be a barefooted, cross-eyed warrior.

Chapter 13

What's a Girl to Wear?

Older women likewise are to be reverent in their behavior, not malicious gossips nor enslaved to much wine, teaching what is good, so that they may encourage the young women to love their husbands, to love their children, to be sensible, ***pure****, workers at home,* ***kind****...*

Titus 2:3-5

Purity

When my children were small, one of my most worn out sentences was, "You can have a sip; just don't backwash." My sisters, there is a perfect way to drink a Coke. You need a Styrofoam cup, lots of small cubed ice, a cold Coke, and a plastic straw. I can't explain it. It's just the perfect Coke criteria. I've never been a good sharer where a perfect Coke is concerned. Oh, you can have one, just not the one I'm currently drinking. The thought of someone else's saliva or food floating around in my soda – or worse, in my mouth – makes me gag. A contaminated Coke is no Coke at all. I want a pure Coke, cold, with ice, in a Styrofoam cup. I wish I were kidding, but it only takes a little backwash to ruin perfection.

It only takes a little sin to make us impure. Generally, in the Bible, purity is defined as virginal or innocent. It also carries the meaning of being free from defilement or impurities. In a word: unpolluted. Older women are to train the younger women to be pure, uncontaminated by the world and immorality. This includes developing a healthy sense of shame (or modesty) and subdued passions (discretion).

Outward adornment for the Christian woman begins with modesty. Inward adornment begins the same way. In 1 Peter 3:2, an unbelieving husband can be won without a word by the behavior of his wife as he observes her *chaste* and *respectful* behavior. The word for *chaste* is the same word, *pure,* in Titus 2:4. Pure behavior begins with cultivating pure thoughts and inclinations. "And do not be conformed to this world, but be transformed by the renewing of your mind, so that you may prove what the will of God is, that which is good and acceptable and perfect" (Ro. 12:2). We prove what the will of God is by our good behavior, but that good behavior begins with pure thoughts. Inner adornment first, then outward adornment.

What kind of thoughts are pure thoughts? Philippians 4:8 gives us help. "Finally, brethren, whatever is true, whatever is honorable, whatever is right, whatever is *pure,* whatever is lovely, whatever is of good repute, if there is any excellence and if anything worthy of praise, dwell on these things." Think on the things that line up with God's word, things that inspire reverence and awe toward God, things that conform to the commands and will of God, things that are free from evil and the world's pollution, things that are pleasing and lovely, things spoken with the good of others in view, things that are morally excellent, and things that are commendable.

In a mom's attempt to help her children think before they spoke, I told my children to pretend that their mind was an airport and that they were air traffic controllers in charge of what planes were allowed to land in their minds (the airport), whether enemy planes or friendly planes[69]. Philippians 4:8 was their missile system. If a thought was true, honorable, right, pure, lovely, good, excellent or praiseworthy, they could give the thought a clear runway on which to land. If it didn't meet the criteria, they were to shoot it down, blow the thought to smithereens with the word of God, and blast it out of their minds.

---

[69] If I'm remembering correctly, Kay Arthur gave this tutorial in her video series many moons ago on the book of Philippians. As a young mom, I was excited to share it with my children. I think it's a timeless help.

Warning: I might be on my soapbox for a minute or so. Hold the tomatoes. What we tell ourselves about the things we see, listen to, engage in – this is what is crucial to remaining pure. For example, if you rationalize that you can watch a series on a streaming service as long as you have your finger on the fast forward button, your *plan* is actually to watch something you know has the capacity to contaminate your mind (or heart), but you've convinced yourself you can control the contamination. Really? Might I suggest we learn to use the "thumbs-down" button? Mark the questionable shows and don't open them back up. We might do some research before we press play. What videos do you watch? What kind of humor is your mind engaged in? Do social media sites suck you in for hours? Hear me. I don't think all entertainment is wicked. I like good art as much as the next girl, old movie buff that I am. Purity demands we do a little prepping.

When we watch or read or listen to any form of media, we should consider what it is doing to our souls. What will we ruminate on after it's over? What images will be in our heads that we can't unsee? What cultural ideas are we swallowing without reasoning through them? How do we feel after we've watched a film? Where do our thoughts go during that particular song? Are we escaping through the books we read? Do we live in them or through them? What about our imagination? Where do we go (in our heads) when we're sad, afraid, tired, bored, lonely, feeling unloved? Is it pure? Do any of these things contaminate our minds? If we are Christians, we have the mind of Christ (1 Corinthians 2:16). Do we want that mind polluted by the world's media trash heap? Mommy porn is taboo for us. If we want a good read with a hero named Christian, read *The Pilgrim's Progress*, not *50 Shades of Grey*. (Stepping off the soapbox… slowly.) It's been my practice (though not perfect) to try to have a ratio of at least twice the amount of God's word than entertainment during a day.[70] What I've found is that it usually ends up being much more Scripture than I planned because the more we eat from the word, the more appetite for it we have.

[70] How do you like me now?

Modesty

We are encouraged to train younger women to be pure with their bodies as well as their minds. This includes modesty, in dress and in action, and teaching the dangers of promiscuity, of fornication, and of infidelity. This includes fidelity not only in marriage beds, but in our heads. (Back upon the soapbox...) Don't be breaking the seventh or the tenth commandment in your head or in your bed.[71] We are meant to teach young women to cultivate beauty in their appearance, but not for the purpose of enticing and flirting. Frankly, I don't want my husband, my sons, and my grandsons (or yours) to see your breasts, your derriere, or your waistline. Men aren't only admiring your tattoo or your piercings. And you, Christian! Stop putting swimsuit pictures on my social media feeds where my husband can see it! (Sheepishly inching back off the box...)

Purification

How do we stay pure? Two of the first verses I memorized, as a new Christian, were Psalm 119:9 and 11: "How can a young man keep his way pure? By keeping it according to Your word." "Your word I have treasured in my heart, that I might not sin against You." To oversimplify, stay in the word and develop a taste for quick repentance. Develop a desire for quick obedience. Don't linger over the choice. Trust God is right and side with Him immediately. Purity demands vigilance. We sometimes talk ourselves into approving a little dirt, sort of the "five second rule" for sin. Just this once. Just for a second. It won't matter. Think of your beautiful wedding dress (imagined or real) with one little ketchup stain on the bodice. It only takes one blemish to ruin the look. Germinate a little sin, cultivate a garden of impurity. A little alien saliva in your Coke is gross.

---

[71] And I might add the sixth commandment, because some women have murdered their spouses in their heads to rationalize having another man in their bed. Stop that! By the way, the commandments are found in Exodus 20.

I'm sad that I can't always say, "Follow my example as I follow Christ." But I'm learning my weaknesses. For instance, I know that if I'm physically having a rough day, I'm more susceptible to the lure of sin. I know that I wound easily, so when I'm offended, I make a concerted effort to forgive quickly and stave off the disease of bitterness. Sometimes I deceive myself into thinking I'm obedient just because I *know* something is true. None of us lives a perfectly pure life. Only Jesus gets that experience. But because we are in Him, we have the power to be pure, and the grace to pull us out of our impurity when we slip. I love Titus 2:11-12: "For the grace of God has appeared, bringing salvation for all people, *training us to renounce ungodliness and worldly passions, and to live self-controlled, upright and godly lives* in the present age." God's grace trains us. The grace that we older women receive from God trains us to train the younger women around us. Renounce ungodliness. Renounce worldly passions. Be pure.

Kindness

My family moved to Ft. Walton Beach, FL[72] when I was a sophomore in High School. It was awkward. I was awkward. I didn't make friends easily. Truth be known, I didn't really try. Friends were risky.

I was enrolled in Mrs. Edwards' English Composition class. She was a lovely, young black woman. And she was so kind. One day, she called our attention to the chalkboard and instructed us to diagram the sentence written there. Not only did I not know how to diagram a sentence, I did not know what a grammar diagram was. I had never seen anything like it. I sat... quietly... wondering why everyone in the room but me seemed to know what to do. And I didn't dare draw attention to my inadequacy. I looked up. She motioned me to the chair next to her desk. In fear and trembling, I got out of my seat and did as she directed.

"Why aren't you working?" she asked. "I don't know what it means to diagram a sentence" was my reply. Mrs. Edwards scribbled the sentence

[72] I actually lived on Hurlburt Field Air Force Base for most of my high school years.

on a notepad and said, "Point to the noun." I pointed. "Point to the verb." I pointed. What other parts of speech do you see?" I told her. After I answered her questions, she looked me in the eye and said, "I will get you some basic worksheets, but you don't need to know this. You know how to construct a sentence. Back to your seat, and don't worry – I will tailor your test."

In the weeks to come, I sat in that chair next to her desk quite a few times until she finally decided to transfer me into a class with less review and more writing. One moment, though, is permanently etched in my memory. I was leaving her class for the last time and she called my name. "Dennie, I have something for you." And she handed me a copy of T. H. White's *The Once and Future King*. I took it from her hand, and she said, "It's yours to keep. Be sure to pop in and let me know what you think of it." It was my first introduction to what I now know is literature. It is marvelously written, and next to my Bible (and maybe Hugo's *Les Miserables*), it is my favorite. I liked to read *before* I met Mrs. Edwards. I loved words *after* Mrs. Edwards. Her kindness changed the trajectory of my world.

Looking back, I think she suspected what a mess of a girl I was. And I truly was a mess. An alcoholic father, sexual abuse by an airman on the base, deeply depressed, deeply ashamed, and deeply lost. Her kindness, and that of two other teachers that year, might genuinely have saved my life. Her kindness proved God's kindness. Though I did not know or serve Him, He ordained the kindness of others to sustain me. I'm forever grateful to Him and for those three teachers.

In the Bible, *kindness* is often translated *good*, but it carries the meaning of being fit or useful. The idea is to show oneself useful and mild, to be fit for use and yet pleasant, and to act benevolently. It is faithfulness expressed through generosity and kindness. You might be shocked to know that this word is found in Matthew 11:30 where Jesus says, "for My yoke is *easy* (kind, fit), and My burden is light."[73]

Kindness is at the very center of who God is. "*Love is patient, love is kind...*" God is love and Love is kind. The Bible exhorts us to be kind to

[73] Think on that for a few days. You're welcome.

one another, all of us, not just women. But it says of the ideal woman, "She opens her mouth with wisdom, and the teaching of kindness is on her tongue." Our kindness is to be in speech as well as conduct. What we say and do needs to fit the other person's need. We commend ourselves as God's servants through kindness (2 Corinthians 6:4-6). It's a kind of stamp that says, "I'm not doing this on my own." Kindness is a fruit of the Spirit, and yet we are told to put it on. It's intentional.

There are several people in the Bible that tender my heart, that make me think of the desperate sophomore in high school that I once was. One of them is Mephibosheth. You can meet him in 2 Samuel 9. David asks, "Is there still anyone left of the house of Saul, that I may show him kindness for Jonathan's sake?" The answer is yes. The answer is Jonathan's son, Mephibosheth, exiled and crippled in both feet. David sends for him and shows him kindness. "Do not fear, for I will show you kindness for the sake of your father Jonathan, and I will restore to you all the land of Saul your father, and you shall eat at my table always." I often wonder about Mephibosheth's reaction to that. Did he hear anything after the word *kindness?* Not sure I would have. But the thought of being invited to the table of the king would have captivated my heart. It's not just kind. It's scandalously kind. And yet that's the kindness we have received, each and every Christian, for God takes us out of our exile and brings us into His kingdom, makes us His sons and daughters, feeds us at His table every Sunday and through His word daily, once crippled, once wandering, now freshly washed with feet tucked up under the tablecloth of the King.

I recall a time when my mother was visiting. She had life-altering health issues, but she wanted to take a drive on Skyline Parkway through Shenandoah National Park. Her disease made travel cumbersome and walking was no less miraculous for her. She needed constant help, used a walker, but was super pleasant. Jon loved her. We decided to have breakfast, drive all morning, and stop for lunch at a restaurant and brewery that Jon and I have enjoyed for several years. Well, until that year. Who knew there would be hundreds of people there? Who knew that they had added pavilions, bars, stages, washhouses, distillery buildings, and shops? Apparently, hundreds of other people knew this. I received no such memo. It was an hour to get seated in the dining room. Bathrooms were standing room only and no toilet paper. I had that "amusement park" feeling that never amuses me much. When Jon saw the crowd, I expected him to shut things down and head for home. He has never liked waiting for restaurant seating or roller coaster rides. Well, honestly, he's not in favor of waiting at all.

But that day, he patiently drove us several hours down the road just to see pretty trees and mountain views. He stopped to take pictures of us in the cold Virginia wind. He waited for an hour + to get a table to eat a meal that was excellent, but cost us more than time. And he did all of that knowing that he had to be back home before 7:00 pm to serve at our church, an hour and a half drive. He managed all of this with joy, not gritting his teeth or glaring at his watch. He smiled, served, and loved my mother and me the entire time. He was kind. She never forgot it. Neither will I.[74]

> *Be kind to one another, tenderhearted, forgiving one another, as God in Christ forgave you. Ephesians 4:32*

> *And the Lord's servant must not be quarrelsome but kind to everyone… 2 Timothy 2:24*

> *I led them with cords of kindness, with the bands of love, and I became to them as one who eases the yoke on their jaws, and I bent down to them and fed them. Hos. 11:4 (ESV)*

> *Take My yoke upon you and learn from Me, for I am gentle and humble in heart, and YOU WILL FIND REST FOR YOUR SOULS. For my yoke is easy and My burden is light. Matthew 11:29-30*

---

[74] Husbands are irresistibly handsome when they love your mother.

This is the kindness we are to offer to others. It's the type that I was offered for a year through a young, lovely teacher. And this is the kindness we teach to younger women. We learn it from the One who has been kind to us. We learn it up close to Him, yoked in union with Him. His yoke is kind, useful, fit to our needs and to the needs of others. Fit actions and fit words. How do we teach it? Be it. This kind of kindness demands that we engage other women, that we stretch out our hands to the one that's a mess – the crippled, exiled one or even the cold, self-sufficient one. We should ask, "Is there anyone to whom I may show kindness?" and then we should be kind. Kind because God is kind to us. Kind because some mess of a girl is desperate for it. Kind because the love of Christ compels us.

Gentle and Quiet Spirit

I think it appropriate to slip Peter's description of a woman's attire into this chapter as well. "Your adornment must not be merely external - braiding the hair, and wearing gold jewelry, or putting on dresses; but let it be the hidden person of the heart, with the imperishable quality of a gentle and quiet spirit, which is precious in the sight of God" (1 Pet. 3:3-4).

When I was a young woman, I wasn't fond of meekness, or what I presumed was meekness. In fact, I felt disdain for any woman who wouldn't stand up for herself. I viewed any woman that appeared gentle as a victim and hated them almost as much as I hated myself. I watched my own mother get "walked on" by my father, and like any damaged teen with dad issues, her peace-keeping and excuse-making angered me even more. As it turns out, I stood up on the inside, time after time, in my imagination, but on the outside, I was docile as a lamb and even more cowardly.

After God drew me to Himself, I beheld Jesus, gentle (meek) and humble, and realized not only was I wrong about my mom, I had completely misunderstood this thing called meekness, confusing it with weakness, cowardice, and impotence. Turns out, it's the opposite.

My mom died only three years ago. She suffered greatly and she suffered well. I asked my husband, "Can you name any woman you know that has a truly gentle and quiet spirit?" I wish he had said, "You do." But no, he said, "Your mom." Early on, when I was that woman I mentioned above, mom was gentle and quiet, but there was a difference in my pre-Christian mom and the mom that I knew once Christ got hold of her. The difference was fear. Her frightened gentleness became "Christ-gentle" and her fear of speaking her mind became "Christ-quiet." Her fear was put in the grave. Christ had embedded into her character a gentle and quiet spirit from an eternal source, one that could withstand difficult relationships and trying circumstances.

A gentle spirit is an "inwrought grace of the soul exercised chiefly toward God. It's that temper of spirit in which we accept God's dealings with us as good and just and therefore, without disputing or resisting. It does not fight against God or struggle and contend with Him.[75] Everything I need, in Christ I possess.[76] Because of this, we have the freedom to be meek and not pusillanimous.[77] Meekness is the fruit of power, the power of the love of Christ in us.

> ***Come*** *to Me, all who are weary and heavy laden, and I will give you rest.* ***Take my yoke*** *upon you and* ***learn from Me****, for I am gentle and humble in heart, and you will find rest for your souls. For my yoke is easy and My burden is light. Matthew 11:28-30*

> *Therefore, I, the prisoner of the Lord, implore you to* ***walk in a manner worthy*** *of the calling with which you have been called, with all humility and gentleness, with patience, showing tolerance for one another in love. Ephesians 4:1*

---

[75] W. E. Vine, *Vines Complete Expository Dictionary of Old and New Testament Words* (Nashville: Thomas Nelson Publishers, 1985).

[76] Thanks again, Cindy.

[77] You gotta love that word, right? For you younger folks, it means cowardly.

> *So, as those who have been chosen of God, holy and beloved,* ***put on*** *a heart of compassion, kindness, humility, gentleness, and patience. Colossians 3:12*

> *But* ***flee*** *these things, you man of God, and* ***pursue*** *righteousness, godliness, faith, love, perseverance, and gentleness. 1 Timothy 6:11*

> *But* ***the fruit of the Spirit*** *is love, joy, peace, patience, kindness, goodness, faithfulness, gentleness, self-control; against such things there is no law. Galatians 5:22-23*

Consider the yoke of Christ. Just to come under it is to be gentle. He is gentle and lowly in heart. We learn that same gentleness from being yoked to Him and voluntarily coming under His rule. I find all the verbs in the above verses fascinating. Come to Me. Take my yoke. Learn from Me. Walk in a manner worthy. Put on… compassion. Flee these things. Pursue righteousness. And, huh? Where did that noun come from? The fruit of the Spirit is… gentleness. Grown by the Spirit. My mind immediately runs to Philippians 2:12-13: "…work out your salvation with fear and trembling; for it is God who is at work in you, both to will and to work for His good pleasure." Looks like a yoke to me. We loosen our stiff necks and come under His yoke, up close and personal with Jesus. He says "walk this way" and by the power of the Holy Spirit, we walk His way. We learn from Him and we become like Him. We refuse to pull against the yoke. We say to Him, "All that You allow is good and just." And in the world, when the rough stuff comes, we see it from inside the yoke and remember that He knows what He is doing. Infinite resources are available to us in Christ; all that we need for life and godliness are in Him. And so, He works in us a fierce gentleness, not a fearful one. Gentleness that truly is the fruit of the Spirit, the fruit of power, and that is completely unoccupied with our own feelings and rights and self-interest or self-protection. We don't have to be somebody, because we are yoked to Somebody, for "when I am weak, then I am strong" (2 Cor. 12:10).

Along with this gentle spirit is a *quiet* spirit. To be quiet, is to be still, undisturbed. It means "to keep one's seat" but not in the sense that you might think. The word is used in the Old Testament as "lame." That's keeping your seat! You are welcome to disagree with me, but I think this is a great picture of a woman's demeanor in the situation Peter has premised. If your husband is unbelieving (unpersuaded by the gospel of Christ), Peter says to keep your seat for truly, you are "lame." You can do nothing to change his heart. So be still. Stay seated. Remember you are under the yoke of Christ and the burden is His. Remember the fruit of His yoke is peace and rest. If you need something to do, pray and wait for direction. Ultimately, to be quiet is to be at peace, submitting to Christ and resting in His sovereign and beautiful will for you (and for your marriage).

Strength and Dignity

To have a gentle and quiet spirit translates to every aspect of a woman's life, not just in the marriage relationship. Life can be hard. When young women watch you deal with the hard things of life, a gentle and quiet spirit appears to on-lookers as *courage*, or as Proverbs 31:25 says it, "strength and dignity are her clothing." Have you seen a woman that is unflappable? We will talk more about suffering in a later chapter, but for now, let's consider just the day-to-day strength a woman needs. Right now, I have a front row seat to a new mom with a baby that screams pretty much all day. She is attempting to work outside the home. She has an unbelieving husband. In fact, she is an unbeliever. She is befuddled by the believing women around her that are thriving under the same hardships. Why aren't they falling apart? Why can't I do this "stay-at-home thing" like others can? Why can she still smile when her finances look worse than mine? To wear the right "clothes" in front of other women, churched or unchurched, is how we preach the gospel from our pulpits (our homes). To wear a gentle and quiet spirit, to wear strength and dignity in the face of struggles and troubles, to wear kindness when we'd rather lash out, to wear purity when swearing seems a better option, these are the things that say to the world, "I am a Christian and Christ is enough."

The word in the Hebrew for *dignity* means *ornament or decoration.* It's also the word sometimes used for *glory*. When I go to my closet, I try to find something that not only suits an occasion, day, or mood, but also to find something flattering. This divine wardrobe, inward as it is, shows the beauty and wonder of Christ and His Bride. It does more than flatter – it brings God glory. Peter says, "a gentle and quiet spirit, *which is precious in the sight of God.*" It's super precious in God's sight. You might be surprised to discover that when Peter uses those words, he truly is saying something weighty. This divine wardrobe, especially under hard circumstances, is of surpassing value in God's sight. It is costly.

Think about the theme of the entire Bible: Kill the dragon, get the girl. The girl, the bride of Christ, was bought at the highest cost. "Knowing that you were not redeemed with perishable things like silver or gold from your futile way of life inherited from your forefathers, but with precious blood, as of a lamb unblemished and spotless, the blood of Christ" (1 Pet. 1:18-19). We were bought with the precious, the valuable, extremely costly, blood of Christ. And because Christ is in you and you have put on Christ, you wear a wardrobe drenched in that same precious blood, and it is very precious in the sight of God. It is true beauty. So, I say strut your stuff and strike a pose on the worldly catwalk. Clothe yourself with Christ and show His beauty in the church and out of it. Your line of clothing is a holy one, provided for you at a precious cost. So put it on and wear it with joy. Put on kindness, purity, gentleness, a quiet spirit, strength, dignity, good deeds (chaste conduct), and all of the other stunning articles of clothing Christ as provided.[78]

Before I close out this chapter, I'd like to return to my mom's example of a gentle and quiet spirit. As I said, in the beginning, she was gentle and quiet in the wrong way. Self-protection and fear ruled her early years (and mine). By contrast though, in her later years I believe she was a true representative

---

[78] Love, joy, peace, patience, goodness, faithfulness, forbearance, self-control, forgiveness, compassion, the armor of God, Christ. Put Him on!

of Jesus' gentle and quiet spirit, of one who was clothed in strength and dignity. She endured tremendous hardship in her later years, yet without whining, complaining, or manipulating. She quietly entrusted herself to God and never seemed to push for her own way or demand her needs be met. She was stunningly beautiful. No one I know danced as well with a walker. I was always staggered by her gratitude. She had gone from fearful to fearless. So repent. Be fearless. Be beautiful. And like her, put on Christ.

Chapter 14

Workers at Home

> *Older women likewise are to be reverent in their behavior, not malicious gossips nor enslaved to much wine, teaching what is good, so that they may encourage the young women to love their husbands, to love their children, to be sensible, pure,* ***workers at home****, kind, being subject to their own husbands...*
>
> *Titus 2:3-5*

Our church is chock-full of women who work at home. I've been a stay-at-home woman since 1985. When women meet me for the first time, they think I've always been this way. They think I was raised in a Christian home with a mom who did what I'm doing. Not so, Tonto. When Jesus found me, I was working as a data processor for a collection agency in Tulsa, OK. Imagine serving an office of twenty-four women who all hate their jobs, get screamed at by hurting people all day long, get paid on commission, overuse "I might not be able to get blood out of a turnip, but you are no turnip," and employ language that would make a soldier blush. The women I worked with wore invisible shields and dared you to fight them. This was my work environment. Surprisingly, I had no desire to do anything else. I was good at my job, made good money, had a great boss and burgeoning independence.

When God broke through to Jon and me, we made a number of course corrections. One of those decisions was to quit my job and stay home with our then nine-month-old daughter. My quitting meant losing more than half of our income as well as relinquishing the one thing that I thought gave me any significance or sense of autonomy.

I know there are many reasons for women to work outside the home. Some choose to out of need. Some are bullied into it by their husbands. Some don't know anything else. Some get their significance from their jobs. Some think they will be bored at home. The problem with this topic is we women tend to focus on the exceptions rather than the rule. Maybe that's a western thing. I don't know. But I'm not going to focus on the exceptions. Difficult cases make bad law. I'm just going to stick to why we should want to be stay-at-home women. It's God's idea, and He's smart.

You'll note that I refer to myself as a stay-at-home *woman*. I don't like the phrase *stay-at-home mom* because it says that motherhood is the only reason for a woman to be a worker at home. The Bible doesn't make that distinction. Yes, it assumes women will be wives and mothers as a rule. Proverbs 31 is the description of a godly wife.[79] Older women train younger women to love their husbands and children. The biblical assumption is that women will marry and have children. Why? Many women think it's just indicative of the culture of Bible times. Sure, but the Bible is still relevant to you and me. The Bible assumes these things because it is the best course for women.[80] Home is where Christian women thrive. No, I have not forgotten the exceptions nor have I forgotten that it's 2024. I'm only attempting to concentrate on what I believe to be the biblical norm.

To be a *worker* means to be a *watcher or keeper* at home. Paul doesn't qualify Titus 2 training as only for married and mothering women. If you are young and single, you still need to be trained. This is with a view to a future marriage, but that's not always the end for women. I have a single niece who has a job and lives in an apartment. She still has to do the full-time job of managing her own household. I have a friend in her seventies who has never been married and never had children. She still has responsibilities at home. Proverbs 31:27 reads, "She looks well to the ways of

---

[79] It's also a description of Jesus' wife, the church. Reread it. It will set you free from Proverbs 31 guilt.

[80] At this point, you might be labeling me a dinosaur. I'm okay with that.

her household and does not eat the bread of idleness." The teachings on marriage, parenting, and working at home are vital for single women who hope to get married, or who never get married. They will be older women someday, reverent influences in the church, and charged with training younger women.

Wise Managers

What, then, does it mean to be a *worker at home?* Women are to be wise managers of their households. This doesn't mean that all women have personalities bent toward homemaking. Many of us don't. These responsibilities must be learned and cultivated. Duties range from meal planning, cleaning, laundry, and schedules to teaching and training children, caring for husbands, caring for aging parents, stewarding resources, bringing food from afar (I'll let you interpret how far), showing hospitality to family, friends, neighbors, and even providing rest. We are gatekeepers, guarding what's allowed in and out of our homes via the front door, television, phones or computers. We are charged by God to do all of these things well, with excellence.

Take another look at that list. Working at home is not for the fainthearted. The world makes jobs "out there" seem more important, as if to say a woman's value increases with greater distance from the kitchen sink. After she died, there was a line in First lady Barbara Bush's on-line biography that read: "She spent the next two decades primarily dedicating her time to being a wife and mother, while volunteering for organizations such as the YMCA and United Way on the side." This made me smile. It covered the years from 1959 to 1979, public life. What did she do before? She married in 1945. She had six children before 1960. Robin, her second child, died at the age of 4 from leukemia. Barbara Bush had thirty-plus years working at home. When she moved to the White House with her husband, she said this in regard to staying out of policy decisions: "I don't fool around with his office (George H. W. Bush) and he doesn't fool around with my household." She took her homemaking skills to the White House, and she ended up majoring in national hospitality. Her later life is what is touted as impressive. I'm more impressed with her endurance in the early years. She loved her children and her family well. Incidentally, she loved her husband well for 73 years.[81] Her working at home, I'm sure, looked much like ours. She apparently understood the beauty of the role. Striking.

There are many challenges for young women who choose to be workers at home. They are real. Some women are naturals and have wanted nothing more all of their lives. Others of us have to work hard at it. These are learned skills. We learn to be self-starters, managing our time well. We learn to strike a balance between busyness and idleness. We have to be intentional about our day, prioritizing without neglecting our family. It's easy to feel forgotten, unappreciated, even taken advantage of, if we let our emotions or self-pity rule. Workers at home also have to guard their own hearts as well as their homes.

Selfishness in a woman doesn't have much chance against a 24-hour job of building a family and home. Daily we are challenged to look past ourselves to those that are in our care, putting our wants and needs at the bottom of the list in order to better serve our families with grace and love. It's a high calling. Each day is a gift to be redeemed and lived with gratitude. Each moment is an opportunity to impact the kingdom of God, to mold character in our children and in ourselves, to take what we are given and use it to give glory to God, to die to self and find real life. This requires a "chin-up" perspective. By this I don't mean a Pollyanna attitude, stiff upper lip and all that twaddle. What I mean is a Godward perspective, one where God is the lifter of our heads, pulling our chins up to stare into His reassuring face to give us help in our daily struggles. We learn to embrace God's standard rather than run from it.

Home As Pulpit

Womanhood, marriage, parenting, working at home – these are all a statement of faith. Elisabeth Elliot, in one of her many books, said this:

---

[81] *Barbara Bush Biography* (The Biography.com website: URL: https://www.biography.com/history-culture/barbara-bush) A & E; Television Networks, 2014.

"The way you keep your house, the way you organize your time, the care you take in your personal appearance, the things you spend your money on, all speak loudly about what you believe. 'The beauty of Thy peace' shines forth in an ordered life. A disordered life speaks loudly of disorder in the soul."[82] In other words, your home is your pulpit. It will vary from home to home, woman to woman, but for Christian women, the home should clearly say, "Jesus is Lord of this place and of me." Our faithfulness really does count. It makes a difference in the kingdom of God and in the world around us. All we do proclaims what we truly believe. Being a worker at home, if we are doing it with faith-filled reliance upon God, proclaims our dependence upon Him and our own death to our futile ways of controlling our own lives. It says God rules in the big and the little. It says we believe that God is all-sufficient for every need. It's a life of hope and promise and purpose and value.

When I first quit my "job" to work at home, I was told I was wasting my talents. At parties and social events when I was asked, "What do you do?" I would usually look for my husband in the room and excuse myself. What woman wants to blurt out what she really believes: "What I do is not enough." I felt "less" than everyone. No matter my answer, if the words left my mouth, they always seemed to fall into a well somewhere. Plunk. As if they had a penny's value. As if *I* had a penny's value. When we don't receive cash as proof we work, we sometimes believe that what we do has no value. And how do we determine the value of our labor? If we trust the world to assign value to our work, we certainly won't get an accurate assessment. The person staring back in the mirror is usually a poor assessor as well. If God assigns the position, shouldn't He determine its worth? At that time, Jon, in an effort to help me understand the importance of my role, had some business cards made for me. They read: "S. Denise Dorminy, Manager. Specializing in interior design, character building, pediatrics, elementary education, culinary creations, organization and management, scheduling, purchasing, counseling, chauffeuring, entertainment and recreation, and

---

[82] Elisabeth Elliot, *Let Me Be A Woman* (Wheaton, IL: Tyndale House Publishers, Inc, 1976).

Biblical instruction. Owner – the Master Builder (God) and CEO – Jon M. Dorminy." He left out "emergency services," but we won't quibble. I gave a few of the cards out in the awkward situations. Heads tilted to the side with disbelief or curiosity, but those cards did the trick.

Then my children went to school full-time. The first question I heard from the women around me was, "Now what are you going to do?" The inference was "now it's time to get a real job" as if I didn't already have one. Or as if my job at home had stopped. John Piper once said, "... mothering and homemaking are huge and glorious jobs. What children need at age one, five, six, fourteen, eighteen is simply amazing, and so is what those needs call forth from a woman's creativity and heart and mind."[83] He was just answering a question, but his answer was super profound. The needs don't stop, and neither does the work in our homes or in our hearts. It's not just about our children. It's about what God calls forth from a woman, what she gives, what she sacrifices, and what she learns by faith.

A momentary rabbit trail: If I had it to do over again, my children would have never gone to public school. Now, in this culture, I would choose to homeschool them or attempt to send them to a private Christian school. I don't get any do-overs. I would like to encourage you not to let the world have your children five days a week if you can avoid it. And really, you can. I hear all of the time, "We can't afford to live with only one income." What *most* people mean when they say that is, "We can't afford to live the way we want to with only one income." Sacrifices can be made. Sometimes we do without the cool toys. Sometimes we eat more chicken than beef. Sometimes we eat more beans than chicken. Sometimes we can't have streaming services and cable or expensive phones and tablets. The world would tell us that we can't live without them. The world lies. Our children matter more than our comfort and entertainment.

When all of my children left our home, the question came again: "Now what are you going to do? Are you going to finally get a job?" When your

[83] John Piper, *Ask Pastor John: Is it okay for mothers to work full time outside the home?* (URL: https://www.desiringgod.org/interviews/is-it-okay-for-mothers-to-work-full-time-outside-of-the-home, 2010)

children are on their own with their own families, this is a huge temptation as well as a terrifying prospect. I'm sixty-two. Should I run out and get another "real" job again? And what's my motivation in doing so? Do I need the money? Could I even *get* a job with no resume? I'm not exactly marketable. Could I manage a job with my health like it is? Could I still be available to offer my family the kind of help they need? I rode that tricycle in a circle until I dug a round grave. Are you aging? Do you sense the urgency creeping in to finally "be someone" or "make your mark" somehow? If I only have (for the sake of argument with a tinge of hope) thirty years of good quality time left, how should I spend it?

I had to ask myself if my job in God's eyes has changed. Most of the women my age who work outside the home say they are saving for retirement, improving their homes, helping their grown kids financially. I don't think it's sinful, and I'm not getting all judgey on you. But sitting in my empty nest,[84] I asked God, "What IS my job now?" I believe the answer was, "It's the same as it was in 1985." It's Titus 2:3-5, 1 Peter 3:1-7, and Proverbs 31:10-31. There are a few more scriptures that come to mind (specific to me), but being a worker at home is no less important now that my children have their own families than it was when they were toddlers. My home, my marriage, my influence as a parent, grandparent and churchwoman, hospitality, teaching, training – these are all my statement of faith. By what I do, I'm telling you what I believe about the God I serve. Elder woman, wherever you work, what belief do your choices preach? And are you able to work a full-time job outside the home and still be a good worker at home? The Bible doesn't teach a woman's *place* is in the home. But it certainly teaches that a woman's pulpit is in the home. Her family and home are her priority.

The truth is, we usually do what we truly believe. As Christians, our behavior should match our belief. No matter what our current status, we have a conundrum to wrestle with (if we haven't already). At some point, we must ask, "What does God's word say about my work? What does God

[84] I've never really used the term "empty nest." I prefer "open nest." We've had person after person, with a need for a place to stay, living in our home for both short and long periods of time. Until this year, we've not had an actual "empty nest."

say about where I work? How does the Bible define my job as a woman, not just as a mom or wife? What do you believe? No matter the exception or defense of either position (inside the home or out), we have to wrench it out with God and with our husband (if there is one). We have to deal directly with Him and consider His plan for us. He gets to decide, not us.

Wise or Foolish – Build or Tear Down

So far, I've covered the *where* and *why* more than the *what* and *how*. Let's go there, shall we? The book of Proverbs begins with two women, one representing folly and one representing wisdom. The entire book gives us snapshots of foolish and wise women.

Seductive and immoral women are foolish women. The Bible describes the woman who is out to get your man as boisterous and flattering (Prov. 2:16-19, 9:13). They are mainly outside of the church, but the church, once in a while, has her own version. Women who are unhappy in their marriages, longing for a man like yours. They forget the covenant of their God and, in their own emptiness, long for better pastures. They dress right on the edge of propriety, showing just enough cleavage to draw an eye. The Bible tells us that the man who follows after her will come to destruction. In one of the churches I attended, a deacon was seduced by another deacon's wife, divorced his wife and married her. Two families were destroyed. The church was devastated. The arms of an immoral woman (or man) hold you tightly as you both fall into death's pit. These sorts of sins never adversely affect just the sinner. They pollute and damage everyone in their sphere. A beautiful woman who lacks discretion is as a ring of gold in a swine's snout (Prov. 11:22).

We can be the ring in the pig's snout in other ways as well. Every Tuesday morning, I meet with a friend at a local restaurant. We've done this for years. For several months, I watched a woman come to the counter. She was what my mother would have described as "put together." The shoes, the suit, the jewelry, the hair. She was stunning. You couldn't help but look her way when she walked in. She was a head-turner, beauty personified. Not immodest. Just lovely. One morning, I was late and found myself behind her in line. She was her usual stunning self, adorned for work, and then it happened. She opened her mouth. Out rolled words that graffiti artists would be ashamed of. My mouth dropped open. She was mean and demeaning. How could something so vile come out of something so lovely? No discretion. A foolish woman. I was sad for her. Don't be her.

A quarrelsome woman is a foolish woman. There are several proverbs that speak to this woman. She's contentious and vexing. The word *vexing* has several implications. A contentious woman is usually an angry woman. But vexing carries the meaning of anger plus annoyance. This word might be where we get the *nagging* woman. She's a woman who irritates and provokes until she gets her way. The Bible says she's like "a constant dripping" and unrestrainable (Prov. 27:15-16; 19:13). It's better to live in a corner of a roof than in a house shared with a contentious woman (Prov. 21:9; 25:24). It's better to live in a desert land than with a contentious and vexing woman (Prov. 21:19). She's never satisfied, never content. She's foolish. Don't be her.

An odious woman is a foolish woman. "For three things the earth is perturbed, yes, for four it cannot bear up: for a servant when he reigns, a fool when he is filled with food, *a hateful* [odious] *woman when she is married,* and a maidservant who succeeds her mistress" (Prov. 30:21-23). Hateful is a good synonym. Odious can be defined as hateful, detestable, highly offensive, repugnant, or disgusting. Other words we might use are unruly or disordered. She has stepped out of her position. She thinks she is calling all the shots. She has attempted to usurp all of the authority in her home. She's a hellion who is bent on resisting God's authority. The New American Standard Bible has chosen a possibly unfortunate translation on first glance. It uses the word *unloved* making the verse seem to mean *hated,* not *hateful.* I have no scholar hat to put on, but a woman who is unloved in her marriage, especially those not bowing to God's authority, are odious. Many hated women are hateful women. I think God abhors men who have disdain for or ignore and mistreat their wives. I feel compassion for the Leah's[85] of the world. But even pain doesn't give us the right to be odious, embittered women. We need to remember who we are actually serving. We lift our heads to Christ, humble ourselves and entrust ourselves to Him. No matter what kind of husband you serve, don't be an odious, foolish woman.

Foolish women tear down their houses with their own hands. Wise women build their homes (Prov. 14:1). Building takes intention. Tearing down doesn't take any planning. "By wisdom a house is built, and by understanding it is established; and by knowledge the rooms are filled with all precious and pleasant riches" (Prov. 24:3-4). To be God's worker at home, He is calling us to build a home that is decidedly Christian. What do I mean by that? I mean we intentionally build a home that proclaims the excellencies of God and His ways. It becomes our statement of faith to all who enter. You want to know what I believe? Look at the home I've built.

Proverbs 31:10-31, for many years, was a thorn in my side. I read it like a to-do list that I could never finish. I bristled every Mother's Day because someone was going to preach from it, and I was going to fall short… again. It was a burden. One day, I asked our heavenly Father a question: "What does your Bride look like?" The Bible answered: "Glorious, no spot or wrinkle or any such thing. Holy and without blemish. She displays the manifold wisdom of God (Eph. 3:10) and is wholly loved by Christ who gave Himself up for her. She is adorned with fine linen, the righteous acts of the saints (Rev. 19:8). She looks like Proverbs 31:10-31." What? I was gob-smacked. The Proverbs 31 woman could be named Lady Wisdom. The perfect bride. There she is, Christ's wife, the Church at work. Just as the bride of Christ is already-but-not-yet-perfect, so is your husband's bride – you – already-but-not-yet-perfect. If you are a Harry Potter fan, we can draw a correlation to the mirror of Erised in J. K. Rowling's *Harry Potter and the Sorcerer's Stone*. The wizard Dumbledore is explaining to Harry how the mirror works. He says, "The happiest man on earth would be able to use the Mirror of Erised like a normal mirror, that is, he would look into it and

---

[85] "Jacob, he loved Rachel. Rachel, she loved him. And Leah was just there for dramatic effect." Rich Mullins, *Jacob and two Women*.

see himself exactly as he is." But others who looked into it saw the "deepest, most desperate desires of our hearts."[86] Christian women who look into the mirror of God's word in Proverbs 31 should see all that they someday will become, all that the bride of Christ will be, which is our deepest desire. Christian women want to be all that Lady Wisdom is. In Christ, we are already her. In real time, we are working it out with fear and trembling. "Beloved, now we are children of God, and it has not appeared as yet what we will be. We know that when He appears, we will be like Him, because we will see Him just as He is. And everyone who has this hope fixed on Him purifies himself, just as He is pure" (1 John 3:2-3).

The Home's Sermon

What kind of *worker at home* is this woman in Proverbs 31? What does her home, her pulpit, proclaim? She has a husband who trusts her. She's a good helper, and does him good. She's industrious. She plans for her household. She's not a sluggard. She does good deeds. She's frugal and prudent and stewards her household well. She's strong and practical. She's thrifty and generous. She's intentional and plans for the future. She's a snappy dresser (see verse 22), linen and purple – righteous and royal. Strength and honor are her clothing. She's joyfully hopeful. She speaks with wisdom and kindness. She guards and watches over her household. Her children and husband like her and praise her. She fears the Lord. She is a worker and her work brings glory to her husband. She's all the things she couldn't be on her own.

Something happens to us around the age of sixty. The road ahead is shorter than the road behind. An undercurrent of urgency surfaces, running through every aspect of life. For me, that urgency led to building meaningful moments. My mom's illness and then her graduation to heaven anchored that urgency in my soul. The words "make this count" played on repeat in my head. What did I do? I went out and bought two 7-foot by

[86] J. K. Rowling, *Harry Potter and the Sorcerer's Stone* (New York: Scholastic Press, 1997), 213.

4-foot tables and 16 chairs. I bought new dishes, 20 place settings all the same design. I bought new silverware, new glassware. I bought a sideboard and tablecloths. I painted and spruced up the dining room. Why? I have three children with spouses and ten grandchildren. If you do the math, I'm now a couple chairs short. We'll figure it out. The point is, when I decided on meaningful moments, I saw my family around the dinner table praying, singing, eating, laughing, telling stories. I thought of my church and wanted them to feel part of my family. I wanted a place to invite them in, to let them experience who we are. I believe that when someone enters my home, they can know a bit about Jon and me and about the God we love and serve. Maybe by the lack of a television on the main floor, they might perceive that entertainment isn't the lifeblood of our home. I hope my dining room and kitchen speak the words fellowship and communion. I hope my living room invites the rest, peace, and comfort that God gives me every day in that room. I hope the rest of our home says "God has blessed us so that we might bless you." And I pray it says to my family: You are important. You are loved. You are a blessing to me. Rest and enjoy.

I've been reading a book entitled *Home Comfort*. Cheryl Mendelson wrote this in her introduction to a hefty "how to" tome:

> *...what a traditional woman did that made her home warm and alive was not dusting and laundry. Someone can be hired to do those things (to some extent, anyway). Her real secret was that she identified herself with her home. Of course, this did not always turn out well. A controlling woman might make her home suffocating. A perfectionist's home might be chilly and forbidding. But it is more illuminating to think about what happened when things went right. Then her affection was in the soft sofa cushions, clean linens, and good meals; her memory in well-stocked storeroom cabinets and the pantry; her intelligence in the order and healthfulness of her home; her good humor in its light and air. She lived her life not only through her own body but through the house as an extension of her*

> *body; part of her relation to those she loved was embodied in the physical medium of the home she made.*[87]

As Christian women it extends even farther. Our home is not just an extension of ourselves, our own personalities, but an extension of who we ultimately serve and glorify. Our life is one of receiving and giving. God blesses and we use those blessings to glorify Him in thanksgiving and praise. A distinctly Christian home says, "God's children live here and God is good to them." By that, I don't mean that every wall in the house has Joshua 24:15[88] prominently displayed. You can if you want, but that's not the point. I'm saying we should keep our homes in such a way as to proclaim God's goodness to us, and that what we do, in word and deed, we "do all in the name of the Lord Jesus, giving thanks through Him to God the Father" (Col. 3:17).

At the beginning of this chapter, I shared with you the dread I felt when someone asked me, "What do you do?" I'd like to encourage you in the practical endeavor of working at home for the glory of God with more from Mendelson's book:

> *Housekeeping requires knowledge and intelligence as well, the kind that is complex, not simple, and combines intellect, intuition, and feelings. You need a memory good enough to remember how things are done, where things are, what the daily routine requires, what everyone in the home is up to as it affects housekeeping, the state of supplies, budgets, and bills. You have to be able to decipher insurance policies, contracts, and warranties, manage a budget, and master the technical language of instruction manuals for appliances and computers. The ability to split your attention in several ways and stay calm*

---

[87] Cheryl Mendelson, *Home Comforts: The Art and Science of Keeping House* (New York: Scribner, 1999).

[88] ...choose for yourselves this day who you will serve... but as for me and my household, we will serve the LORD.

> *is essential. You need to exercise creative intelligence to solve problems and devise solutions: efficiency measures that save money or time; psychological or social measures to improve cooperation; steps to improve physical comfort; analyses of why and how some routines break down. Housekeeping comprises the ability to find, evaluate, and use information about nutrition, cooking, chemistry and biology, health, comfort, laundry, cleaning, and safety. Above all, housekeeping must be intelligent so that it can be empathetic, for empathy is the form of intelligence that creates the feeling of home. Good housekeepers know intuitively what needs to be done in their homes because they know how their homes make people feel.*[89]

It really does take some God-given smarts to manage a home. And some God-given power to do it in faith, love, and joy. Ms. Mendelson is not far from the kingdom of God in her description, if she's not already in it. But if we take what she says and use our Christian lens, the truth is simply this: everything we do in our homes has consequence, so it should be done in Christ. We steward God's money. We care for our families through meals and laundry and linens and disinfectants. We make our homes comfortable and inviting, our tables generous and meals nutritional and just downright tasty, and we create the feeling of home not with empathy, but by the Spirit of God empowering us to see beyond ourselves to the goal of loving others and glorifying Him with what He has provided. Intelligent? Absolutely. But add faith and we have something altogether grander than what the world can provide.

"Charm is deceptive and beauty is vain, but a woman who fears the LORD, she shall be praised. Give her the produce of her hands, and let her works praise her in the gates" (Prov. 31:30-31). I've never been great at these sorts of things. The produce of my hands has not always praised me in the gates, nor at the dining room table, truth be known. Yet as I've learned

[89] Ibid. Mendelson.

(and continue to practice) my job as a woman in the kingdom of God, I find delight in the trying, in the obeying, in the small steps of faith that somehow get God's holy nod. Maybe just a little delight, especially when it comes to scrubbing the tub,[90] but I'm growing in my understanding of God's goodness to me and what it means to glorify Him in every moment of life. Not a bad gig. Wherever you work, I hope you'll consider the high calling that waits for you at home. God doesn't despise it. Neither should you.

[90] I bought a drill and some brush attachments for it. I now scrub my tub and tiles with a power drill. Life just gets better and better!

Chapter 15

Yes, God is Good... but Good to Me?

Strength and dignity are her clothing, and she smiles at the future.

Proverbs 31:25

How great is Your goodness, which You have stored up for those who fear You, which You have wrought for those who take refuge in You, before the sons of men!

Psalm 31:19

"Do you believe I am good?" It was as if Jesus had popped into my car. I was praying. I said, "Lord, of course I believe You are good." And then, "Do you believe I am good to you?" Oh, now that is a whole different thing, isn't it? I wanted to say, "Of course!" but the words wouldn't leave my mouth. I had to think on it. I mulled it over for weeks, truth be told. In fact, I still ask myself that question when things seem to go awry. It's a good diagnostic. Consider it for yourself. Is God good? Is He good to you? On what do you base your answer? Is He good to you only when things are going well? Is He good to everyone else but You? How can He be good to you and let *that* happen?

That day my thoughts went back to an angry young Christian at a women's retreat in Oklahoma. I had gone to a break-out session on the topic of suffering. The precious woman giving the talk was describing life like a tapestry. You've probably heard the illustration. God is weaving a tapestry with your life. All we see is the back side of it. Knots and hanging threads and messes and pain. At the end, God will reveal to us the other side, the beautiful tapestry of each life. My internal response was something like, "Yeah, yeah, ya-da, ya-da. True for you, maybe." I didn't stay to hear the end. I grabbed my things and went to the woods.[91] I was a disrespectful 30-year-old brat, angry at God for saving me "late." I was stamping my foot, accusing God of not loving me like He loved everyone else. I truly believed God created me "unlovable," so it was impossible for anyone to love me well. I thought God must have made me for the sole purpose of ridicule and abuse. My "tapestry" was ugly on both sides and on purpose. I don't advise encounters like this with the Living God, but in a clearing in the woods, I screamed and threw an unholy fit in His presence. I ended up a sobbing heap on the ground.

But God was merciful to me. He didn't give me what I deserved. No she-wolves came out of the dark. The ground didn't open up. "Oh, give thanks to the LORD, for He is good! for His mercy endures forever" (Ps. 106:1, NKJV). Goodness and mercy. Between sobs, I grabbed my Bible and opened it to Job 40. Flashlight on, I read these words, "Will the fault-finder contend with the Almighty? Let him who reproves God answer it." I read chapters 40-41. The gist of my understanding was: "Who do you think you are? I am God. You are not." Romans 9:20 says, "On the contrary, who are you, O man, who answers back to God? The thing molded will not say to the molder, 'Why did you make me like this,' will it?" My words became Job's words:

> *I know that You can do all things, and that no purpose of Yours can be thwarted. Who is this that hides counsel without knowledge? Therefore I have declared that which I did not understand, things too wonderful for me, which I did not know.*

---

[91] My apologies to that teacher for my abrupt exit. I was rude. Please forgive me.

> *Hear, now, and I will speak; I will ask You, and You instruct me. I have heard of You by the hearing of the ear, but now my eye sees You; therefore I retract, and I repent in dust and ashes"* (Job 42:1-6).

Certainly not every wrong belief I had was righted that night. But I recognized God's sovereignty and His goodness could hold hands.

What was my beef with God back then? He did not protect me from some horrible things in my past. He did not give me a loving father. I knew He could have done something. He could have stopped the emotional bleeding. I blamed Him. Incidentally, He was big enough to handle it. I think I was just angry that affliction and suffering still seemed to be part of the Christian package. We do live in a sin-sick world. We have real enemies – the world, Satan, sin, and our own flesh. But all God's "ways are just; a God of faithfulness and without injustice. Righteous and upright is He" (Deut. 32:4). Psalm 23:6 proclaims, "Surely goodness and lovingkindness will follow me all the days of my life, and I will dwell in the house of the LORD forever." A professor I met many years ago told me the Hebrew is more exciting than our English versions. He said it could be rendered, "Absolute goodness and lovingkindness will chase me down and catch me every single day of my life." He's right. I've been caught over and over and over again by God's goodness and love.

Suffering is packaged many different ways. Bryan, my big brother, was faced with a failing kidney brought on by a series of compounded mistakes. His kidney disease ramped up to the point that he was placed on a kidney transplant list. We prayed for healing. We prayed for donors. And God did a hard and merciful thing. Bryan's son, Matthew, only 32 and faced with some hard circumstances as well, stepped into the shower one evening, fell, and a few days later died, all the result of a brain aneurism. My brother received his son's kidney. An impossibly severe mercy. How do you get your head around that one? Bryan would have given his own life to bring Matthew back. Instead, God arranged life this way. Bryan is still here (much to our joy), living faithfully for God who faithfully afflicted him and delivered him. Matthew is with Jesus, free of all sin and pain. We don't always get to choose our suffering package.

But some we choose. Some of it is our own fault. God's word is full of warnings against foolishness and rebellion. The way of the transgressor is hard, and many times we prove it to ourselves. We get ourselves into all kinds of scrapes simply by ignoring the wisdom of God's word, the gentle whisper of the Spirit's "don't do that." Should we be surprised that God would let us endure the consequence of our fool-hearted choices? "For what credit is there if, when you sin and are harshly treated, you endure it with patience? But if when you do what is right and suffer for it you patiently endure it, this finds favor with God" (1 Pet. 2:20). Did you catch that? We can do what is wrong and suffer for it, and that would be our just reward. Or we do what is right and suffer for it. In that case, when we patiently endure it, Jesus Himself is our reward.

Consider Job

Day 1 – The Sabeans attacked and took all of Job's oxen and donkeys and killed his servants. Fire "from God" fell from heaven and burned up the sheep and his servants. The Chaldeans raided, stole his camels and killed his servants. A great wind came and struck the house that all of his children were in and killed his ten children. Talk about your no-good-horrible-very-bad-day!

Day 2 – Job was afflicted with sore boils from head to foot. His wife told him to curse God and die.[92] God is clear about where this suffering came from. "...and he still holds fast his integrity, although you [Satan] incited Me [God] against him to ruin him without cause." Satan got permission. "Behold, all that he has is in your power, only do not put forth

[92] Which incidentally gives us a clue of who she was listening to: "But put forth Your hand now and touch all that he has; he will surely curse You to Your face" (Satan to God, Job 1:11) and "However, put forth Your hand now, and touch his bone and his flesh; he will curse You to Your face" (Satan to God, Job 2:5). Job's wife to Job: "Do you still hold fast your integrity? Curse God and die! (Job 2:9) Job's wife was on the wrong side. This is not the way to cheerlead your husband through his grief and pain, ladies.

your hand on him." "Behold, he is in your power, only spare his life" (Job 1 and 2). Suffering, whether we brought it on ourselves or were blindsided by it, or whether we understand it or not, is first filtered through the fingers of God. He is not surprised by what you go through. He is not bound to explain it to you either. Suffering is a tool used by a skillful, divine, sovereign Surgeon to make you, Christian, into the image of the One who suffered and died for you. It's part of the Christian package. Let me prove it to you:

> *Before I was afflicted I went astray, but now I keep Your word. Psalm 119:67*

> *It is good for me that I was afflicted, that I may learn Your statutes. Psalm 119:71*

> *I know, O LORD, that Your judgments are righteous, and that in faithfulness You have afflicted me. Psalm 119:75*

> *It is for discipline that you endure; God deals with you as with sons; for what son is there whom his father does not discipline? But if you are without discipline, of which all have become partakers, then you are illegitimate children and not sons… All discipline for the moment seems not to be joyful, but sorrowful; yet to those who have been trained by it, afterwards it yields the peaceful fruit of righteousness. Hebrews 12:7-8,11*

Here are other scriptures you might want to tuck in your heart: Psalm 119:50, 92, 107; Philippians 1:29; 2 Corinthians 4:17; Hebrews 5:8; 2 Corinthians 1:3-5; 2 Timothy 3:12; Matthew 5:10.

For the Christian, many trials are because God faithfully disciplines us as His children. Like Christ who "learned obedience through what He suffered," we are in the same training program. Why do I bring up this topic of suffering in a chapter on God's goodness? Because when the rough stuff piles up and trials come like waves of the sea, one upon another, and we struggle to get our breath, we are tempted to doubt the goodness of our God. We respond with a "why?" upon a "why?" upon a "why?" God can seem silent and cold to our situation. And He's not.

Waves have hit me over the past 15 years. Some of them were waves of loss and grief, loved ones dying and friends deserting. Some of them were waves of betrayal and slander. Some waves came from unexpected places, even from within the church. Some of them were the result of my own sin. Some of them were physical. When I look around me, I am certainly not alone. The waves are hitting everyone, Christian and unbelieving, like the storms that hit the house on the sand and the house on the rock. Some of my trials have simply come from stupidity. Like the time I ate old rice from my fridge and ended up with food poisoning. My suffering was my fault. I learned and rice no longer sits in my fridge for more than two days. All of our trials have purpose. Sometimes God lets us in on that purpose. Sometimes not.

Shame and Suffering

I wrestle with shame on a regular basis. God has been good to heal me of so much misplaced shame, but it still causes a stumble here and there. Shame, although it shows up during suffering, is not a good bedfellow. I'll just dive into the humility pool and share one of God's more humorous lessons:

There once was a butterfly catcher
on a porch, jar open to fetch her.
Unbalanced she fell
through the screen with a yell
for no one was there to catch her.

I was attempting to "save" a butterfly, the old "catch and release" with a jar and a lid. I stretched too far and took a tumble through the already damaged screen of our back porch. It was about a four-foot drop. I tumbled into the flower bed and rolled into the yard. I couldn't repeat this acrobatic wonder if you begged. I still can't figure what I hit my chin on. Between the bleeding gums and the small bleeding gash, the black soil from the flower pot that lost its life, and the grass stains, I was a sight to behold. Go ahead and laugh. I'm over it. But I'm extremely grateful for the lack of video.

I'm not sure what other people think when they fall through a screen into their flower beds, but my first thought was, "Did anybody see me?" At least my neighbors weren't barbequing. I laid in the grass for a few moments, but the urgency for invisibility outweighed my injuries. I dragged myself to my knees, got to my feet, and limped into the house. My second thought was, "I think I'm bleeding." Then I thought, "Jon's not going to appreciate the new door I put in the screen." To his credit, he was gracious after the initial "what the heck?" moment. Once bandaged, I was left to feel the full force of the injuries and the unwarranted shame. I've learned that misplaced shame is a form of suffering on its own. It has to be dealt with quickly. I snapped a little video to one of my friends – the one I knew I could trust to share both in the pain and the ridiculousness of the situation. I took a picture and sent it to another friend who I suspected would laugh and help me to keep the whole thing in perspective. On the ground outside, shame was sitting right next to me. There was no real reason to feel ashamed, but there it was screaming at me to get up and hide the whole debacle. It followed me around most of the day with words like "man, no one does stupid things like that." In fact though, most of us do. Hiding never works. The way to defuse the discomfort of shame is to bring it into the light. So I talked to God about it, and I called some friends.

Shame is debilitating. It's a weight, a ball and chain. Nose dives off porches can be God's means of teaching us out of our shame. God taught me through my porch dive that shame is still hanging on, but I don't have to hang on to shame. Believe it or not, I was encouraged. We learn obedience by what we suffer. Sometimes we even get a little extra wisdom. I've taken a vacation from saving butterflies. I mean, after all, I made a way of escape for them. You're welcome, flutterbugs.

Suffering Well

Though it's not specifically mentioned in the Titus 2 verses we have been examining, a godly woman, one that is strong and dignified, one that senses that her gain is good and laughs at the future, understands the goodness of God and faces trials, pain, grief, suffering, temptations and shame with courage and endurance. She suffers, and she suffers well. The Bible gives us the schematics for hard things and hard times.

> *Consider it all joy, my brothers, when you encounter various trials, knowing that the testing of your faith produces endurance. And let endurance have its perfect result, so that you may be perfect and complete, lacking in nothing.* James 1:2-4

> *In this you greatly rejoice, though now for a little while, if necessary, you have been distressed by various trials, so that the proof of your faith, being more precious than gold which perishes though tested by fire, may be found to result in praise, glory, and honor at the revelation of Jesus, and though you have not seen Him, you love Him, and though you do not see Him now, but believe in Him, you greatly rejoice with joy inexpressible and full of glory.* 1 Peter 1:6-8

> *...but we also exult in our tribulations, knowing that tribulation brings about perseverance; and perseverance, proven character, and proven character, hope; and hope does not disappoint, because the love of God has been poured out within our hearts through the Holy Spirit who was given to us.* Romans 5:3-5

Maybe you noticed the plan as you read. Did you note the *joy* floating around in all of those verses? Did you see the *proof* of genuine faith? Did you see the need for endurance? More importantly, did you see God's hand in the tough times? If you are a Christian, trials are purposeful. They mean something. They accomplish much. This is the cycle for the Christian who lets suffering do what suffering is meant to do:

> SUFFERING (trials, temptations, persecutions) →
> TESTING OF FAITH (Is it genuine?) →
> PRODUCES PERSEVERANCE (endurance/patience) →
> FAITH PROVED GENUINE (perfect, complete, hopeful) →
> REJOICING (exulting in Christ, maturity) →

We move through this cycle over and over throughout our lives. Tragically, we tend to short-circuit the cycle on our own. You can guess where. Instead of *perseverance,* just replace it with your own sinful response when your faith is tested. Ingratitude? Outrage? Insecurity? Worry? Anger? Selfishness? Shame? And then let the dominos fall. What's the result? Yeah, I've been there many times. It's not pretty. Instead of considering it all joy when we face various trials, we consider it something else: an injustice, a crime against us, a punishment, an outrage, a distraction, a frustration, an undeserved wound. We don't consider from Whose hands it came, so it's just something that happens. Life isn't fair. The dominos of self-preservation start falling after that.

God has given us some incredibly helpful footholds when the climbing is hard and the winds are ruthless:

One foothold is simply this: God really is good. Not just good, but good to you.

> *Good and upright is the LORD; therefore He instructs sinners in the way. Psalm 25:8*

> *For the LORD God is a sun and shield; the LORD gives grace and glory; No good thing does He withhold from those who walk uprightly. Psalm 84:11*

Bless the LORD, O my soul, and all that is within me, bless His holy name. Bless the LORD, O my soul, and forget none of His benefits; who pardons all your iniquities, who heals all your diseases, who redeems your life from the pit, who crowns you with lovingkindness and compassion; who satisfies your years with good things, so that your youth is renewed like the eagle. Psalm 103:1-5

The Lord is good to all, and His mercies are over all His works. Psalm 145:9

Foothold 2: God has a purpose in everything He allows. He doesn't waste suffering, sorrow, pain, grief, troubles. No – in Christ they mean something. And if they mean something to Him, they should mean something to us. If he is saving your tears in a bottle (Psalm 56:8) and your prayers in a bowl (Revelation 5:8), you can be certain, Christian, that nothing you face is lost and wasted. He's your redeemer, after all. He has no dark side. He doesn't send a wave of suffering your way with a snarky grin and a "let's see how she likes this!" He doesn't get some sick pleasure over your pain. It is His pleasure to afflict us in the sense that it is His pleasure to do His good and perfect will for His glory and for our good. And it will be His great pleasure to see our suffering end someday. John Piper wrote about the death of Jonathan Edwards who died away from home from an inoculation for smallpox. Edwards' wife, Sarah, heard about his death and sent a letter to her daughter Esther. It read: "My very dear child! What shall I say? A holy and good God has covered us with a dark cloud. O that we may kiss the rod, and lay our hands on our mouths! The Lord has done it. He has made me adore His goodness, that we had him so long. But my God lives; and He has my heart. O what a legacy my husband, and your father, has left us! We are all given to God; and there I am, and love to be. Your affectionate mother, Sarah Edwards."[93] Sarah understood God's goodness and

[93] John Piper, *The Pleasures of God* (Portland, OR: Multnomah, 1991). Quoted from *The Works of Jonathan Edwards* by Dwight Sereno.

she knew God had a purpose, not only in the death of her husband, but in her husband's legacy to her family. There is so much more to our suffering than meets the eye.

Foothold 3: We are not alone in our suffering. A friend of mine delights to say that "what God brings us to, He brings us through."[94] I sometimes wish He would just take me out of it. How about you? He has been known to do that. But the majority of the time, because the suffering has purpose, He lets it have its perfect result. That takes time. That requires our obedience, our coming under the yoke of His purpose and plan. God says to us in our troubles the same as He said to Joshua, "Have I not commanded you? Be strong and courageous! Do not tremble or be dismayed, for the LORD your God is with you wherever you go" (Josh. 1:9). I've asked many, many times for God to take away the chronic illness that I struggle with. I've had the elders of my church anoint me with oil and pray for me. My church prays for me every single Sunday, sometimes to my chagrin. Though I would love for Him to take this from me, I've reached the "this is mine" stage. If God refuses to remove it, then it must be from His hand. If it is from His hand, it has been given to me. I believe my response then is to steward it as a gift from Him. His word on the subject is clear:

> *"My grace is sufficient for you, for My power is made perfect in weakness." Most gladly, therefore, I will rather boast about my weaknesses, so that the power of Christ may dwell in me. Therefore I am well content with weaknesses, with insults, with distresses, with persecutions, with difficulties, for Christ's sake; for when I am weak, then I am strong. 2 Corinthians 12:9-10*

God is with me in my weakness. He is with me by His Spirit. He is with me through the grace of His church toward me. He is with me in the pages of His word.

---

[94] Thank you, Linda.

Foothold 4: Every trial will make me look more like Christ. We can be certain we will be that much closer to looking like the One who saved us. Because of His goodness in our suffering, we will change for the good in Christ. Our lives will glorify Him, and we will be changed from glory to glory. Look again at 2 Corinthians 12:9-10. Boast in our weaknesses? Yes, so the power of Christ may rest upon us. We will endure trials and our endurance will prove our faith is genuine. Well-content with weaknesses, with infirmities? Yes, for Christ's sake, and because when we are weak, then we are strong.

To be well-content (some versions say "take pleasure"!) in our sufferings is a seeming conundrum. We can "take pleasure" in our suffering, or be content in them, by thinking well of God who sent them or allowed them. I have to know God is good. I have to believe that what God allows in my life is good and good for me. This reminds me of gentleness which we have already studied. To be meek, if you remember, is "to accept God's dealings with us as being good and just without disputing or resisting." Boiled down, we can think of suffering as right and good, and choose to reassure ourselves that God is good. "Why are you downcast, O my soul? Hope in God." Receive the thing *without disputing, without resisting, and I would add without mumbling or grumbling.*

Is this easy? I don't think so. But in Christ it can and is done. It is an issue of lifting our heads and looking in the face of Christ, perceiving His goodness and choosing to respond in gratitude. Murmuring and complaining in the face of suffering, and considering it unjust, is to call God unjust. It is to be discontented with His goodness. It is to say to God, "I deserve more than this." Ingratitude is a stench in the nostrils of God. I'm understanding this more and more as I get older. I recall a verse in Deuteronomy 28:48-49,

> *Because you did not serve the LORD your God* ***with joy and gladness of heart, for the abundance of everything,*** *therefore you shall serve your enemies, whom the LORD will send against you, in hunger, in thirst, in nakedness, and in need of*

> *everything; and He will put a yoke of iron on your neck until He has destroyed you.*

I don't know. Seems like God puts a high value on obedience *with gratitude*. Suffering can either be our friend (received with gratitude, stewarded with faith and obedience, given room to make us into the image of Christ who sent the trial in the first place) *or* our enemy (given reign to steal from us the abundance God promised, to lie to us with empty words of instant gratification and pleasure, to tempt us to think we deserve more or that God is not good, to slip the yoke of iron over our necks and lead us to destruction). Frankly, we get a yoke either way.

Again: "Come to Me, all you who labor and are heavy laden, and I will give you rest. Take My yoke upon you and learn from Me, for I am gentle and lowly in heart, and you will find rest for your souls. For My yoke is easy and My burden is light" (Matt. 11:28-30). We get to choose. The heavy yoke of iron that comes from being enslaved to our own desires – wanting what we want when we want it without regard to God's will, *or* this yoke, the yoke of Christ. You say, "I don't want a yoke at all." Then you just chose the one of iron. According to Jesus, His yoke is easy, not "easy-peasy." It means it is *kind*, it fits us. The yoke God puts on me is not the same yoke you wear. The one I wear fits me. It's for my good. Yours is fit for you and is for your good. His burden is light. Why? Because He carries the lion share. He manages the weight. He puts on us what is needed for us and for His purpose. He is gentle – that same fruit we talked about above. He is lowly in heart, humble by choice. He gives rest to His yoke-wearers. The yoke of Christ goes to the child of God with her hand out. We are to take it. We are to learn from Christ. We do what He does, and in terms of suffering, it's been spelled out for us:

> *For to this you were called, because Christ also suffered for us, leaving us an example, that you should follow in His steps: "Who committed no sin nor was deceit found in His mouth"; who, when He was reviled, did not revile in return; when He*

> *suffered, He did not threaten, but committed Himself to Him who judges righteously; who Himself bore our sins in His own body on the tree, that we, having died to sins, might live for righteousness – by whose stripes you were healed. For you were like sheep going astray, but have now returned to the Shepherd and Overseer of your souls. 1 Peter 2:21-25*

Christ left us an example to follow. We can entrust ourselves to Him who judges righteously, to Him who knows what's best for us and those around us, to Him who knows what "rod" we need to kiss. Joyfully, gladly, with gratitude… we can boast about our weaknesses because God's grace is enough, more than enough, and the power of Christ dwells in us and is perfected in all of our weaknesses. How? It's none of our business. It's His business how it all works for His glory. We've been given an example and He is enough. Why can we rejoice in fried car transmissions, in cranky washing machines, in wet phones in the rice bag, in loneliness, in betrayals, in sullied reputations, in diabetes, in cancer, in loss, and in death? Because Jesus. His grace is sufficient. He has done everything for us. He can do anything in us. Everything we need, we have in Him. Maybe each trial *is* His grace to us. I think it all turns on whether we believe He is good. Consider it all joy and endure, Christian. The power of Christ will not only rest upon you, it will "rest you." His goodness and mercy will chase you down and catch you every day of your life.

Chapter 16

Barefoot and Cross-Eyed Again

> *Therefore, since we have so great a cloud of witnesses surrounding us, let us also lay aside every encumbrance and the sin which so easily entangles us, and let us run with endurance the race that is set before us, fixing our eyes on Jesus, the author and perfecter of faith, who for the joy set before Him endured the cross, despising the shame, and has sat down at the right hand of the throne of God.*
>
> *Hebrews 12:1-2*

We've come full circle. Christian women are beautiful. Glorious. Caryatids in the household of God. We each are privileged to be one of them. We are here to prove the beauty and worth of God in all things. Every good thing in life, every gift, every virtue, every work, is meant to glorify Christ and Him crucified. Every bad thing God graciously turns for good is meant to glorify Christ. We are meant to prove His beauty and infinite value in everything we say and do. Like Abraham Kuyper said, "There is not a square inch in the whole domain of human existence over which Christ, who is Sovereign over all, does not cry, Mine!"[95] Jesus has claimed your heart, your mind, your soul, your body, your family, your home, your career, your leisure, the city you live in, the state you reside in, the country you call home, and every other inch of the earth, and beyond. You are owned,

[95] Abraham Kuyper, *Sphere Sovereignty (1880)* in *Abraham Kuyper: A Centennial Reader*, ed. James D. Bratt (Cambridge: Eerdmans, 1998).

paid for with the blood of Christ, and every jot and tittle of your life was redeemed to cry "Glory!" to God. This is what Titus 2 is saying about you as a Christian woman. Let your attitude, your speech, your emotions, your will, your love, your family, your home, your hospitality, all of your works... let them cry "glory!" to your Lord.

Every Sunday Christians are called by God to join with the church to worship God. We all do this in various denominations and in different ways. The congregation I worship with participates in a covenant renewal service, or the Lord's Service, each week. We take the call of God seriously. He calls us to Himself. We show up. It's our joy and privilege. After the call, we corporately confess our sins. Christ washes our feet. We stand clean, in full assurance of faith that we are forgiven. At this point, we are consecrated, set apart as living sacrifices to God. The Lord "cuts us up" by the word of God. We hear His word spoken over us and to us and we are changed. We then share the covenant meal with Christ and one another, eating the bread and drinking the wine, singing in joy, we "pass the peace," greeting one another in the peace of Christ, experiencing the fullness of communion. Then finally, we are commissioned and sent forth to proclaim the excellencies of Christ in the world until the next Sunday. It's beautiful, isn't it? Call, confession, consecration, communion, commission. This is our Sunday worship. *And*, in a micro sense, it can be our everyday worship.

What if this worship is the daily duty of the Christian? What if this is, like Romans 12 calls it, our daily spiritual service of worship that proves the will of God as good, acceptable, and perfect? What if this is the context in which every woman (and man) of God grows? Every morning the sun rises and we are called by God out of the grave of sleep, wakened because His mercies are new every morning and He is faithful. Our bare feet hit the ground and we are reminded of our dependence on Christ. We humbly confess our need and our sin and we stand forgiven, ready to embrace all that God has foreordained for us this day. Throughout the day, He consecrates us, cutting, molding, shaping, using His word and all of life to sanctify us in the truth. Throughout the day we pray and commune with Him, trusting Him by faith to sustain and keep us, to persevere us and make us like Himself. And we are sent out into the world as heralds of the good news of Christ's rule. Called out and called back, in and out throughout our day, lying down at night to await tomorrow's resurrection to life again. Every day the beat of repent, believe, repent, believe, is beneath the call, confession, consecration, communion, and commission, like a heart-beat, reminding us Who gave us life and Who sustains it. This liturgy is a day in the life of God's subjects, God's children.

Where is the a, b, c, 1, 2, 3? It's within vigilant, purposeful, intentional faith. Do you believe God is good? Do you believe God is good to you? Do you believe God is training you with His grace? He is at work in us, both to will and to do His good pleasure. He has started a work in us and He will complete it. We are God's workmanship created in Christ Jesus to do good works which He has prepared in advance for us to walk in. Respond in faith, intentionally entrusting yourself to God who is good to you, believing what He says to you, taking off the old and putting on the new, letting Him turn your desires into His desires. Intentional, childlike faith. Before you go to sleep, pray. Plan your obedience. Don't let each day just "happen." Tonight, by prayer and faith, plan for an obedient tomorrow. When you are called forth from sleep, repent of any desires you have to change the plan to fit your own wants, and entrust yourself to God, humbly submitting to His plan for the day. When you veer off the path, repent and commune with Him. Submit to His goodness when the day looks like it wasn't planned at all. The surprises that hit us are never surprises to Him. Understand that your days are fit for your good and His glory.

The world we live in is desperate for Christian women to joyfully and boldly proclaim and manifest that God's will for women is not some slavish, unfulfilling, waste of time and talent. Too many of us are looking outside of our husbands, our churches, and our homes for the silver-bullet to make us somebody special. Look! Look into the mirror of God's word and see that you are already enough. You are a child of the king – daughter of the Most High, chosen before the foundation of the world to be conformed into the very image of the One who loves you and redeemed you. Is there any job higher than that? Any role better than that?

God's women are kingdom builders and dominion takers. What does this look like practically? Yes, we clean the floors. Wash the dishes. Change diapers. Fix fabulous meals. Play with our children. Teach our children. Shop for clothes and groceries. Do the laundry. Bandage knees and elbows. Read books. Read the Bible. Open our homes to friends and family. Take a meal to someone in need. Pray. Sing. Worship. Love. And so much more. And we do it all kindly, joyfully, gratefully, diligently, excellently, contented and in an attitude of submission to Christ, all with a view to love and holiness. We know everything is His: what we do, what we think, what we want, who we are. Our homes are our pulpits, and we shout the gospel from our doorsteps with the fruit of the Holy Spirit and our deeds. "Look what God has done in us, in our families, through our families, for our families! Look, world, how the very grace of God has saved me and trained me to deny my own passions and to live sanely, righteously, and godly! He has done it! Witness the joy of a waif, purchased with the highest price, the blood of Christ, to serve at the pleasure of the King! Even witness my struggles, my failures, my sufferings, my sins, and see that I am still dancing over the corpses of my enemies (flesh, sin, Satan, the world), taking ground in the kingdom, and slowly but certainly being conformed to the image of Jesus Christ!" With a steady beat of turning from sin and turning to God, we are becoming reverent, truth speaking, self-controlled, teachers of good. We are loving our husbands and loving our children well. We are growing into sensible, pure, workers at home, kind women, subject to those in authority over us, not dishonoring God's word. We are becoming purveyors of strength and beauty, fearing the Lord, gentle and quiet, bold and glorious. Perfectly? Not yet. But...

Every morning before feminine feet hit the floor, listen for the heavenly rhythm. Repentance. Faith. Repentance. Faith. Repentance. Faith. Not quitting. Young or old. Barefooted and cross-eyed until the earth is full of the knowledge of the Lord as the waters cover the sea. Barefoot and cross-eyed Christian women until He comes or until we are called home.

Special Thanks

To my husband, Jon – Thank you for forty years of locking arms and facing hard things, for comforting me in my fear, for encouraging me through weakness, for being patient when others wouldn't, for not scoffing when others appeared to, and for loving me beyond what I deserve. You still send me.

To my mighty men, Jonathon and Luke – Thank you for esteeming me beyond my worth. The men of God that you have become proves out that God's grace is lavish over ill-equipped moms. Proverbs 10:1 says "A wise son makes a father glad, but a foolish son is a grief to his mother." Neither of you has ever been a source of grief. You both are wise, and your father and I are glad. May you always know and believe that I am your greatest admirer. I love you both "this much, all the way around." It's a skoobily-doobily promise.

To my daughter, Shanna – Thank you for being the loudest cheerleader in my world. I am proud to call you my favorite daughter and my best friend. May the words in this book remind you how wonderful you are. You don't realize it, but when I grow up, I want to be brave and beautiful and kind like you. I am your greatest admirer too – and I love you "this much, all the way around." It's a skoobily-doobily promise.

To Rachel and Kayla – Thank you for remembering my frame and loving me anyway. And thank you for being beautiful "Ruths" to my imperfect "Naomi". My sons and grandchildren will rise and call you blessed. And so do I.

To my grandchildren – Olivia Joy, Kuyper Whitefield, Ezra Josiah, Elijah Levi, Jane Browning, Anselm Leland, Ransom Knox, Amos Augustus, Josephine Agnes, and Henry Kalmar (and any more to come) – thank you for engendering in this heart of mine more love than I ever believed possible. You are each my very favorite and I love you.

To Cindy, Linda, Kay, and Pam – Thank you for listening to me drone on and on about this thing and yet loving me along. You are true encouragers, listeners, and confidants. You are friends indeed and more precious than you can know.

Thank you to Trinity Reformed Church in Martinsburg, WV for your consistent prayer on my behalf. It is a privilege to worship with you all.

Thank you to the crew at Chick-fil-a (especially Kendra) who allowed me to use the dining room as my writer's cabin, with a refreshed Coke in a Styrofoam cup, lots of ice, a straw, and smiles all around. Ya'll are awesome!

Thank you to those who actually believed there was a book in me somewhere. You know who you are and your faces were ever before me in the writing.

Recommended Reading:

The Supper of the Lamb
by Robert Farrar Capon

Let me Be A Woman
by Elisabeth Elliot

Women of the Old Testament and *Women of the New Testament*
by Abraham Kuyper

The Ten Commandments: A Guide to the Perfect Law of Liberty
by Peter J. Leithart

Home Comforts: The Art and Science of Keeping House
by Cheryl Mendelson

The Lord's Service: The Grace of Covenant Renewal Worship
by Jeffrey J. Meyers

Overcoming Sin and Temptation: Three Classic Works
by John Owen

Rediscovering Holiness: Know the Fullness of Life with God
by J. I Packer

Taking God Seriously: Vital Things We Need to Know
by J. I. Packer

Weakness is the Way
by J. I. Packer

This Momentary Marriage: A Parable of Permanence
by John Piper

Heaven Misplaced: Christ's Kingdom on Earth
by Douglas Wilson

To a Thousand Generations: Infant Baptism –
Covenant Mercy for the People of God
by Douglas Wilson

Personal Declension and Revival of Religion in the Soul
by Octavius Winslow

Printed in the USA
CPSIA information can be obtained
at www.ICGtesting.com
CBHW061254110924
14403CB00012B/625